ACCA AA

Audit and Assurance

First edition 2007, Twelfth edition January 2018

ISBN 9781 5097 1659 3

e-ISBN 9781 5097 1689 0

British Library Cataloguing-in-Publication Data
A catalogue record for this book is available from the British Library

Published by

BPP Learning Media Ltd
BPP House, Aldine Place
142–144 Uxbridge Road
London W12 8AA

www.bpp.com/learningmedia

Printed in the United Kingdom

Your learning materials, published by BPP Learning Media Ltd, are printed on paper obtained from traceable sustainable sources.

The contents of this book are intended as a guide and not professional advice. Although every effort has been made to ensure that the contents of this book are correct at the time of going to press, BPP Learning Media makes no warranty that the information in this book is accurate or complete and accepts no liability for any loss or damage suffered by any person acting or refraining from acting as a result of the material in this book.

BPP Learning Media is grateful to the IASB for permission to reproduce extracts from the International Financial Reporting Standards including all International Accounting Standards, SIC and IFRIC Interpretations (the Standards). The Standards together with their accompanying documents are issued by:

The International Accounting Standards Board (IASB) 30 Cannon Street, London, EC4M 6XH, United Kingdom.
Email: info@ifrs.org Web: www.ifrs.org

Welcome to BPP Learning Media ACCA **Passcards for *Audit and Assurance***.

- They **focus on your exam** and **save you time**.
- They incorporate **diagrams** to kick start your memory.
- They follow the overall **structure** of the BPP Study Texts, but BPP ACCA **Passcards** are not just a condensed book. Each card has been separately designed for clear presentation. Topics are self-contained and can be grasped visually.
- ACCA **Passcards** are still **just the right size** for pockets, briefcases and bags.

Run through the **Passcards** as often as you can during your final revision period. The day before the exam, try to go through the **Passcards** again! You will then be well on your way to passing your exams.

Good luck!

For reference to the Bibliography of the *Audit and Assurance* Passcards please go to: www.bpp.com/learningmedia/bibliographies

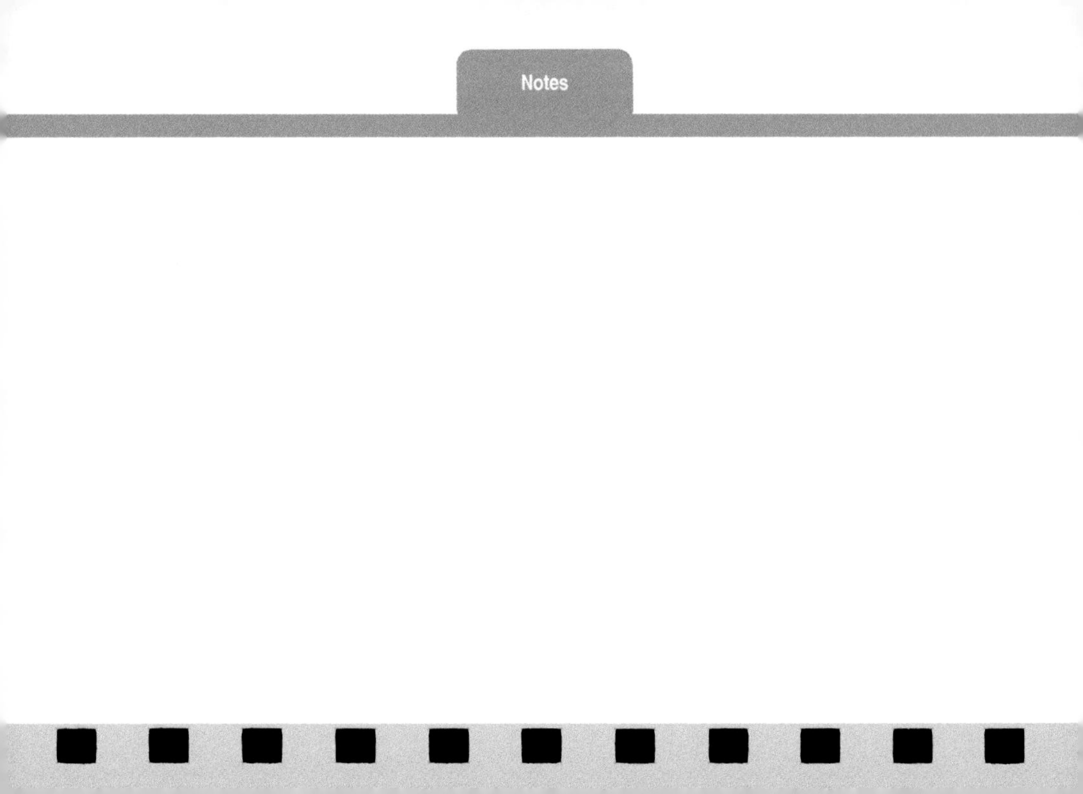
Notes

1: Audit and other assurance engagements

Topic List

The purpose of assurance services

External audit

Assurance and reports

The chronology of an audit

This chapter provides an introduction into why there is a need for assurance services, such as external audit and review. It is important that you have grasped the key auditing concepts outlined in this chapter because it is the foundation for the rest of your studies.

You may not be examined specifically on these issues, but will need to understand them to answer other questions later on.

There are various people interested in the financial statements of a company. They are called **stakeholders**.

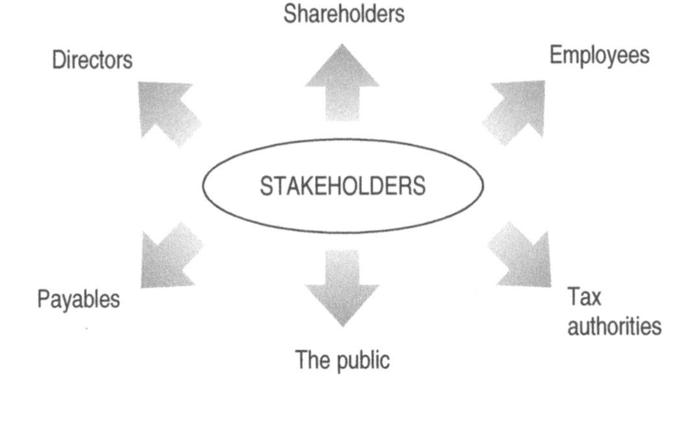

Particularly in larger companies, the **owners of a company and the management of that company are distinct**.

Directors are **accountable** to the shareholders in their role as **stewards** and **agents**. Accountable means being required to justify actions and decisions.

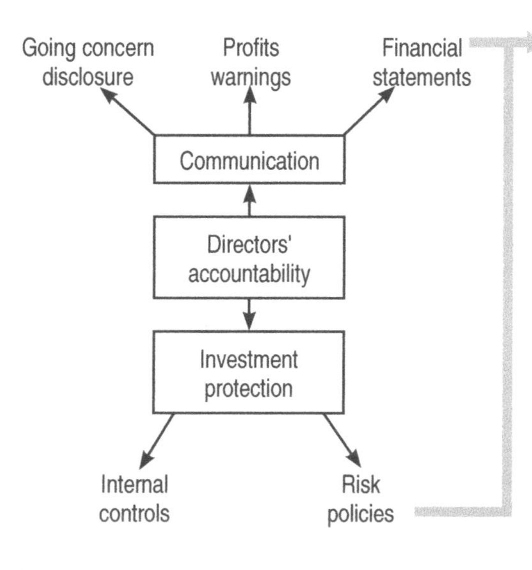

These issues are often discussed under the umbrella title **corporate governance**.

Corporate governance is the system by which companies are directed and controlled. Good corporate governance ensures that stakeholders with a relevant interest in the company's business are fully taken into account.

The UK government has made recommendations as to what constitutes good corporate governance in various codes. These have been adopted by the Listing Authority for the Stock Exchange in the form of the **UK Corporate Governance Code**. This is discussed in more detail in Chapter 3.

A key consideration for directors is **management of risk** and **internal controls**.

Audits or reviews can give stakeholders a degree of assurance concerning these issues.

An **audit** is an exercise whose objective is to enable auditors to express an opinion whether the financial statements (FS) are prepared, in all material respects, in accordance with an identified financial reporting framework. The phrases used to express the auditor's opinion are '**give a true and fair view**' or '**present fairly, in all material respects**' which are equivalent terms. (ISA 200: para. 3)

Fair presentation requires the faithful representation of the effect of the transactions, other events and conditions in accordance with the definitions and recognition criteria for assets, liabilities, income and expenses set out in the applicable Framework.

Auditors do not bear any responsibility for the **preparation and presentation** of the financial statements, which is the **responsibility of the directors**.

Exam focus

There are many misconceptions about the role of the auditors, which are referred to as **'the expectations gap'** (the gap between what auditors do and what people think they [should] do).

Statutory audits are required by law for most companies (small and dormant companies may be exempt). Various other bodies require an audit under law, including: building societies, trade unions, some charities.

External v internal audit Larger entities often have internal audit. Internal auditors act as a control. Their work can benefit the external auditors.

The objective of a **review engagement** is to enable an auditor to give an opinion on whether anything has come to his attention that would mean the FS were not properly prepared/true and fair, **on the basis of procedures which would not constitute an audit**.

The external audit can be distinguished from review engagements by the level of assurance provided.

Engagement	Type of assurance provided	Examples
External audit	Reasonable	Statutory external audit
Review	Limited	Review of interim financial statements

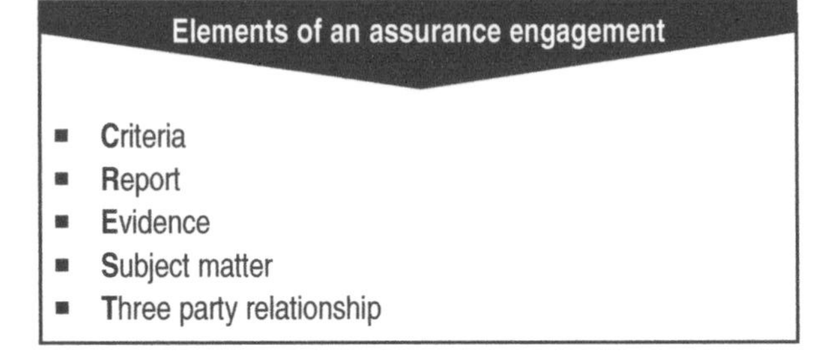

Reasonable assurance is not a guarantee of correctness, but an assurance of truth and fairness within a reasonable margin of error.

Materiality is the expression of the relative significance or importance of a particular matter in the context of the FS as a whole. A matter is material if its omission or misstatement would reasonably influence the decisions of the addressee of the auditor's report. It has both qualitative and quantitative aspects. (ISA 200: para. 6)

Limitations of an audit

- Not purely objective
- Not all items in FS checked
- Limitations of systems
- Chance of collusion in fraud
- Time lag (period – reporting)
- Limitations of the auditor's report

Chronology of an audit

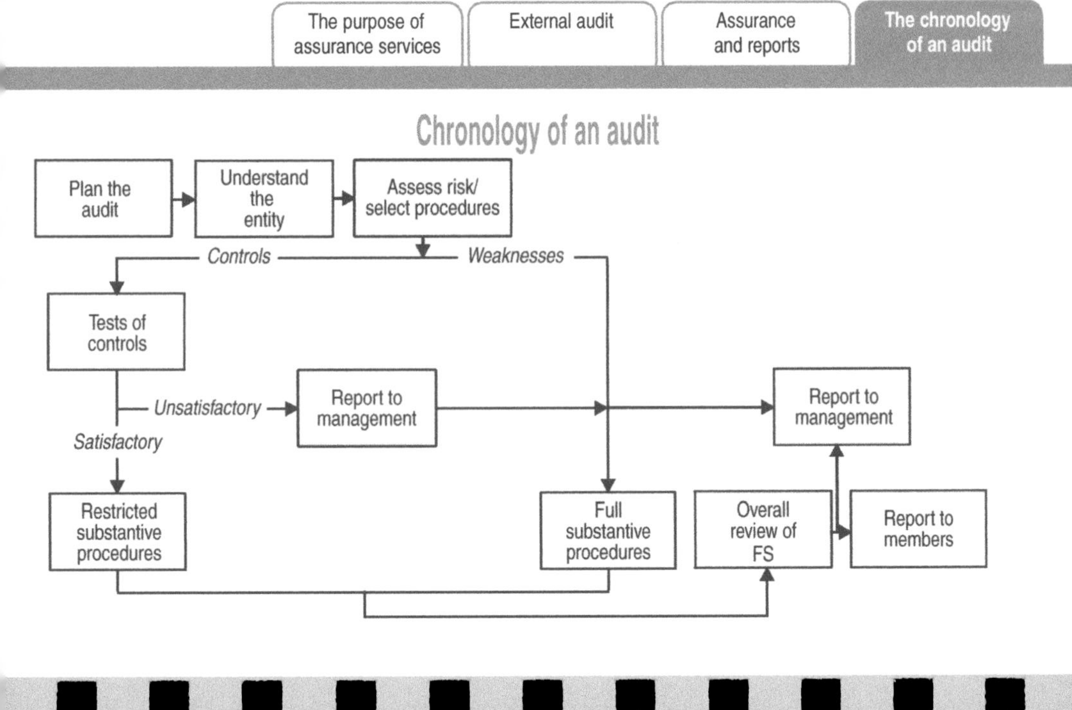

2: Statutory audit and regulation

Topic List

- Statutory requirements
- Audit regulation
- Rights and duties
- International Standards on Auditing

This chapter contains essential background knowledge about the regulation of auditing. Auditing is self-regulating in the UK, the government having devolved this duty to the recognised supervisory bodies (RSBs), of which ACCA is one. This may not necessarily be the case in other countries. It also looks at the authority of ISAs.

The details in this chapter could be examined either in isolation or in conjunction with the topics contained in Chapter 4 on professional ethics and appointment.

Most limited companies are required to have a statutory audit. There are some exemptions, one of which is small entities.

A **small entity** is any entity in which:

(a) There is concentration of ownership/management in a small number of people, and

(b) One or more of the following are also found:

  (i) Few sources of income and uncomplicated activities

  (ii) Unsophisticated record-keeping

  (iii) Limited internal controls and potential for management override of internal controls

  (iv) Few personnel, many having a wide range of duties (IFAC, 2016)

The statutory opinion – UK example

Explicit opinions

The auditors give an **opinion** as to whether the FS are **true and fair**, or present fairly.

This is generally taken to mean that accounts:

- Are factual
- Are free from bias
- Reflect the commercial substance of the business's transactions

They also report on the consistency of the directors' report.

Implicit opinions

- **Adequate accounting records** have been kept and **returns adequate** for the audit have been received from branches not visited.
- The **accounts** are in **agreement** with the **accounting records** and returns.
- **All information** and **explanations** have been **received** that the auditors think necessary.
- **Details** of **directors' emoluments** and other benefits have been correctly **disclosed** in the FS.
- **Particulars of loans** and other **transactions** in favour of **directors** and others have been correctly **disclosed** in the FS. (Companies Act 2006: s. 498)

Note. In the UK there are extra reporting requirements for auditors of companies appying the UK Corporate Governance Code and/or ISA 701 *Communicating Key Audit Matters in the Independent Auditor's Report*.

UK

Various associations exist, such as ACCA/ICAEW. Stringent entry requirements/codes of ethics.

Eligibility

This is likely to be directed by national law. It should ensure that audits are only done by people with suitable qualifications and experience.

In the EU, people carrying out audits must have the permission of the relevant authorities. In the UK, the relevant authorities are the RSBs (associations such as ACCA).

There should also be **supervision** and **monitoring** of auditors by the national regulatory body. Inspection would depend on various factors, such as the size of firm and the number of audits carried out.

The regulatory body should expect to see commitment to technical excellence and ethics.

The overriding duty of the auditors is to report on the truth and fairness of the FS. This is a duty owed to shareholders.

In the UK, the Companies Act 2006 provides the auditors with **statutory rights** as well:

Statutory rights

- A **right of access** at all times to the books, accounts and vouchers of the company.
- A **right to require** from the company's officers such **information and explanations** as they think necessary for the performance of their duties as auditors.
- A **right to attend any general meetings** of the company and to receive all notices of and communications relating to such meetings which any member of the company is entitled to receive.
- A **right to be heard at general meetings** which they attend on any part of the business that concerns them as auditors.
- A **right to receive** a copy of any **written resolution proposed**.

(Companies Act 2006: s. 499 & 502)

IFAC is the International Federation of Accountants, based in New York. IFAC co-operates with member bodies from around the world to initiate, co-ordinate and guide efforts to achieve international technical, ethical and educational pronouncements for the accountancy profession.

The **International Auditing and Assurance Standards Board** (elected from members of the IFAC) issues **International Standards on Auditing** (ISAs). ISAs are specially written to try to incorporate the differences which will exist between accounting under various national laws.

They do not override national law, but if national law conflicts with the best practice in an ISA, member bodies of IFAC from that country are required to encourage a change in the law to conform to the ISA.

IAASB Pronouncements

- International Standards on Auditing (ISAs)
- International Standards on Review Engagements (ISREs)
- International Standards on Assurance Engagements (ISAEs)
- International Standards on Related Services (ISRSs)
- International Standards on Quality Control (ISQCs)
- International Auditing Practice Notes (IAPNs)

Authority of IAASB pronouncements

- ISAs are applied in the **audit** of financial information.
- ISREs are applied in the **review** of historical financial information.
- ISAEs are applied in assurance engagements other than the audit and review of historical financial information.
- IAPNs provide practical assistance to auditors.

Exam focus

Chapter 2 of your Study Text includes a list of ISAs examinable in F8, as well as other examinable documents.

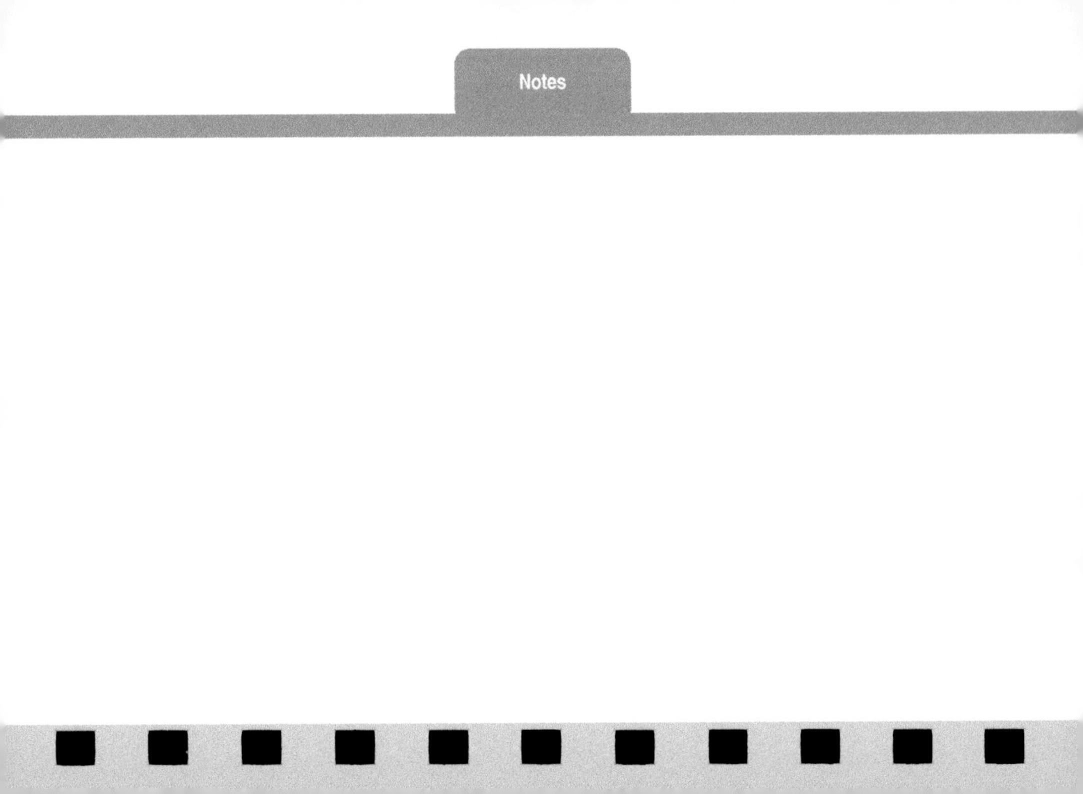
Notes

3: Corporate governance

Topic List

- Corporate governance
- Codes of best practice
- Audit committees
- Internal control effectiveness
- Communication with those charged with governance

This chapter discusses the importance of good corporate governance within a company and the aims and objectives of audit committees.

The topic of corporate governance could be examined in conjunction with internal audit (Chapter 5) in a scenario question.

Corporate governance is the system by which companies are directed and controlled.

The problem of corporate governance

The problem of corporate governance arises because often in companies (particularly larger ones) management and owners are not the same people. The managers (stewards) of the company report to the owners. Other people use that report to draw conclusions about the company.

This 'report' (the financial statements) is audited by auditors, who report on its truth and fairness.

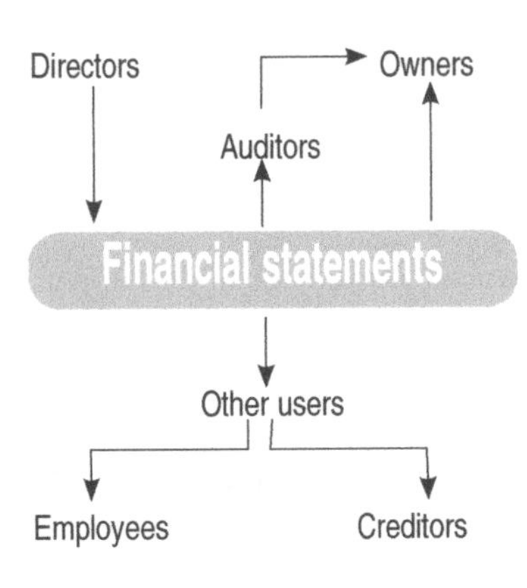

Exam focus

An audit committee is one corporate governance tool. You could be asked to discuss the benefits of having an audit committee

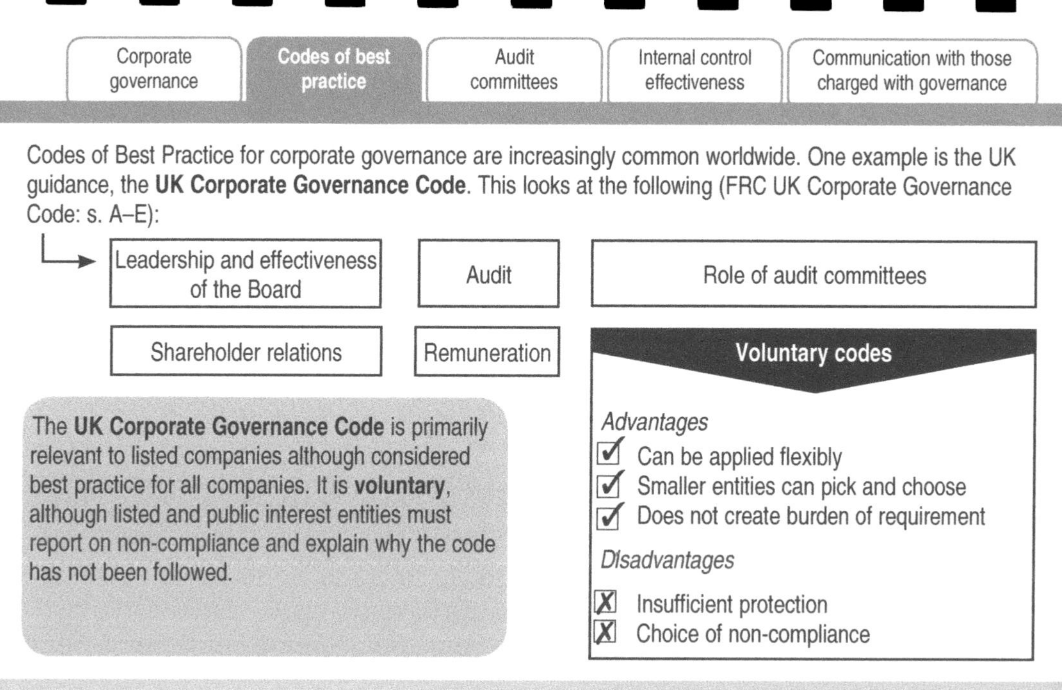

Codes of Best Practice for corporate governance are increasingly common worldwide. One example is the UK guidance, the **UK Corporate Governance Code**. This looks at the following (FRC UK Corporate Governance Code: s. A–E):

- Leadership and effectiveness of the Board
- Audit
- Role of audit committees
- Shareholder relations
- Remuneration

The **UK Corporate Governance Code** is primarily relevant to listed companies although considered best practice for all companies. It is **voluntary**, although listed and public interest entities must report on non-compliance and explain why the code has not been followed.

Voluntary codes

Advantages

- ✓ Can be applied flexibly
- ✓ Smaller entities can pick and choose
- ✓ Does not create burden of requirement

Disadvantages

- ✗ Insufficient protection
- ✗ Choice of non-compliance

The Board

- Meet regularly
- Balance of execs/non-execs
- Some non-execs to be independent
- Rigorous/transparent nomination process
- Directors to submit for re-election (FRC UK Corporate Governance Code: s. B.1, B.2 & B.7)

Chairman

- Roles of Chairman/Chief Exec to be distinct (FRC UK Corporate Governance Code: s. A.2.1)

Internal controls and risk management

- Board should maintain sound risk management and internal control systems. (FRC UK Corporate Governance Code: s. C.2)

Audit committee

- Should be established (FRC UK Corporate Governance Code: s. C.3.1)

Internal audit

- Consider the need for the internal audit function annually (FRC UK Corporate Governance Code: s. C.3.6)

Remuneration

- Formal transparent process for setting reasonable remuneration (FRC UK Corporate Governance Code: s. D.1)

Relations with shareholders

- Ensure satisfactory dialogue with shareholders. (FRC UK Corporate Governance Code: s. E.1)

Auditors

- Required to report on whether UK listed companies comply

OECD Principles of Corporate Governance (OECD, 2015)

- Promote transparent and efficient markets, and consistent with law
- Protect shareholders' rights
- Equitable treatment of all shareholders
- Encourage co-operation between corporations and stakeholders
- Timely and accurate disclosure on all material matters
- Accountability to company and shareholders

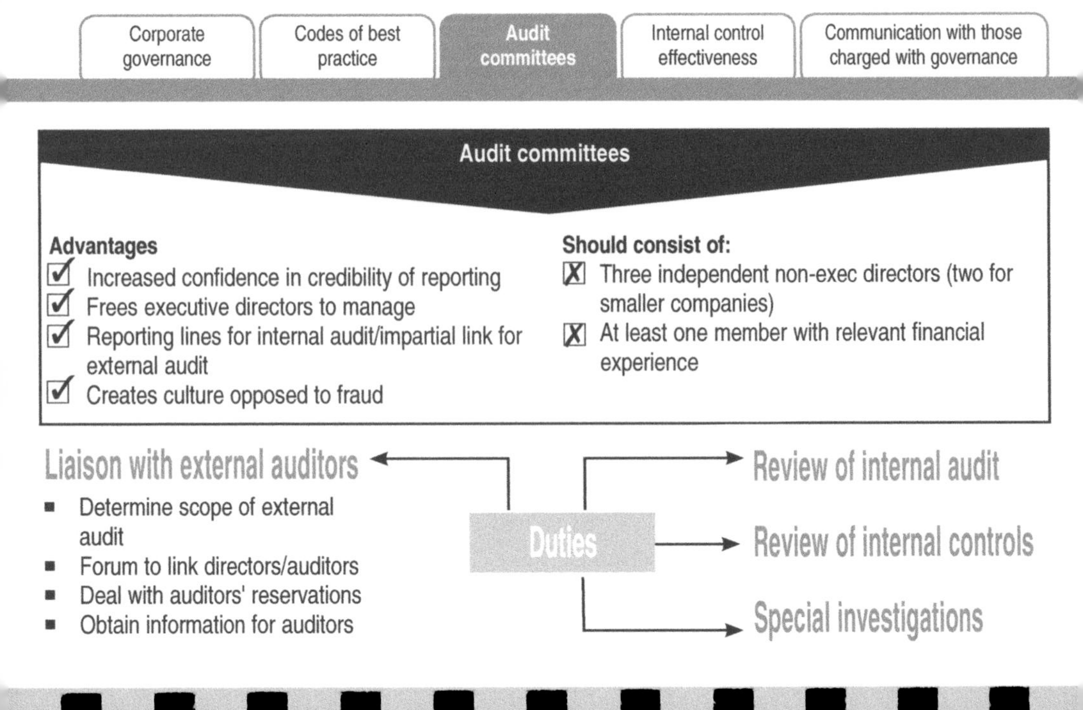
Audit committees
Advantages
Increased confidence in credibility of reporting
Frees executive directors to manage
Reporting lines for internal audit/impartial link for external audit
Creates culture opposed to fraud
Should consist of:
Three independent non-exec directors (two for smaller companies)
At least one member with relevant financial experience
Duties
Liaison with external auditors
Determine scope of external audit
Forum to link directors/auditors
Deal with auditors' reservations
Obtain information for auditors
Review of internal audit
Review of internal controls
Special investigations

Directors

Internal controls and risk management are very important in fulfiling directors' duties to the shareholders, which are:

- To safeguard the assets
- To prevent and detect fraud

Protect the investment of the shareholder

Therefore they:

- Set up a system of internal control
- Review its effectiveness
- Consider the need for internal audit

Auditors

As part of their audit:

- Ascertain controls
- Review controls
- Evaluate controls
- Determine audit approach based on controls

Can also offer services:

- To review controls
- Report to shareholders

as a function separate from audit

ISA 260 *Communication with Those Charged with Governance* provides guidance.

The objectives of communicating are to:

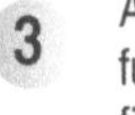

1. Assist in **understanding** audit-related matters and develop a constructive working relationship
2. Obtain **information** relevant to the audit
3. Assist those charged with governance to fulfill their **responsibility** to oversee the financial reporting process

Matters to be communicated

- The auditor's responsibilities in relation to the audit
- Planned scope and timing of the audit
- Significant findings from the audit
- Auditor independence (listed entities) (ISA 260: paras.15–17)

4: Professional ethics and quality control procedures

Topic List

The ACCA's Code of Ethics and Conduct *is a key topic area.*

When approaching questions on ethics, follow a three-stage strategy:

- *What do the fundamental principles say?*
- *What does the detailed guidance say?*
- *What does my common sense/practical experience tell me?*

Professional ethics is likely to be examined in a scenario situation so you will have to apply your knowledge to the particular facts in the question.

Quality control is also an important topic area.

Code of Ethics and Conduct

This lays out ACCA's rules stating the ethics and behaviour required by all **members** and **students** of the ACCA. Guidance is in the form of **fundamental principles** (see below), specific guidance and explanatory notes.

Integrity	Members shall be straightforward and honest in all business and professional relationships.
Objectivity	Members shall not allow bias, conflicts of interest or undue influence of others to override professional or business judgements.
Professional competence and due care	Members have a continuing duty to maintain professional knowledge and skill at a level required to ensure that a client or employer receives competent professional service based on current developments in practice, legislation and techniques. Members shall act diligently and in accordance with applicable technical and professional standards when providing professional service.
Confidentiality	Members shall respect the confidentiality of information acquired as a result of professional and business relationships and should not disclose any such information to third parties without proper or specific authority or unless there is a legal or professional right or duty to disclose. Confidential information acquired as a result of professional and business relationships should not be used for the personal advantage of members or third parties.
Professional behaviour	Members shall comply with relevant laws and regulations and should avoid any action that discredits the profession.

(ACCA *Code of Ethics and Conduct*: s. 100.5)

A member's objectivity must be beyond question if he/she is to report as an auditor. That can only be assured if the member is, and is seen to be, independent.

Risks

The ACCA provides **specific guidance** on:

- Undue dependence on an audit client. If total fees from a client that is a public interest entity exceed 15% of the firm's total fees for two years in a row the firm must:
  - Disclose this to those charged with governance
  - Arrange an independent pre/post-issuance review

  (ACCA *Code of Ethics and Conduct*: s. 290.217)
- Overdue fees
- Actual/threatened litigation
- Associate firms: influences outside the practice
- Family and other close personal relationships
- Beneficial interest in shares or other investments
- Voting on audit appointment
- Loans to and from clients
- Goods, services and hospitality

The *Code of Ethics and Conduct* identifies the following risks to independence and objectivity:

- **Self-interest**
- **Self-review**
- **Advocacy**
- **Familiarity**
- **Intimidation**

(ACCA *Code of Ethics and Conduct*: s.100.12)

Example

A key risk to independence arises from the provision of other services to audit clients. An auditor:

- Must not assume a management responsibility
- May not prepare accounts for a public interest entity
- Must not review his own work
- Cannot be an employee of an audit client

Safeguards against loss of objectivity

- Quality control procedures
- Audit committee
- Partner rotation

The benefit of partner rotation is that loss of independence through familiarity is guarded against. In practice it is not popular because of the loss of trust and experience built up. If an individual is a key audit partner for seven years for a public interest client, they must be rotated off the audit for two years.

The professional duty of confidentiality

Exam focus

Information gained from professional work should not be disclosed unless:

- Consent obtained from client
- It is required by law
- A professional right/duty to disclose

- A member should not use (or appear to use) information for his own or some other's benefit.

Exceptions to the prohibition on disclosure

Disclosure

Obligatory

- Member knows or suspects that client is involved in **treason, drug trafficking** or **terrorist offences**.
- Under **ISA 250** when NOn-Compliance with Laws And Regulations (NOCLAR) causes material misstatements in FS.

Voluntary

- Disclosure is reasonably necessary to **protect** the **member's interests**.
- Disclosure is compelled by **process of law** (say in an action where member must give evidence).
- It is in the **public interest** to disclose.
- Some **government bodies** have **statutory powers** to compel disclosure.

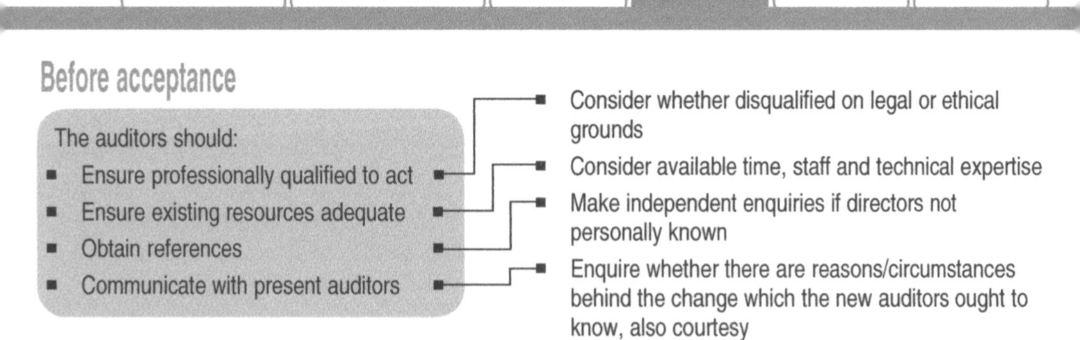

After acceptance

The auditors should:

- Ensure outgoing auditors' removal/resignation properly conducted
- Ensure the new auditors' appointment is valid
- Set up and submit a letter of engagement

Appointment decision tree

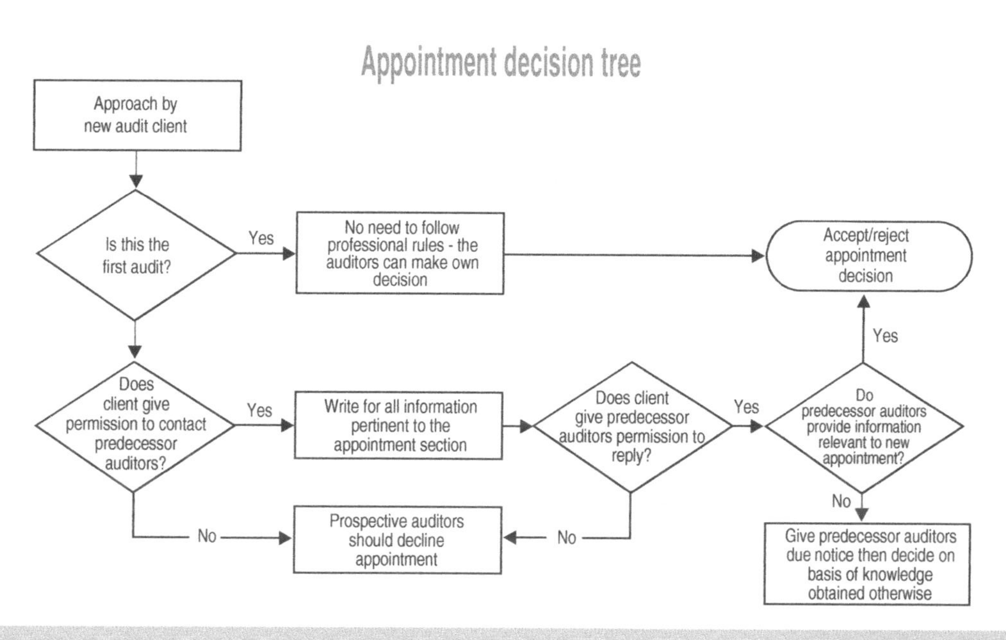

Advertising, publicity and obtaining professional work

Members

- Should not obtain or seek work in an unprofessional manner.
- Can advertise, but should have regard to relevant advertising codes/standards.
- Should not make disparaging references to/comparisons with the work of others.
- Should not quote fees without great care not to mislead.
- Should not offer fees, commission or reward to third parties for introducing clients.

Audit fee

The audit fee is a sensitive issue. It is estimated according to charge-out rates and work planned.

Lowballing is offering audit services at less than the market rate; undercutting others in a tender.

It can be an independence threat as such a fee is less than the work is worth. However, audit does have a fluctuating market price and firms can reduce fees.

Client screening

As part of the tendering process, audit firms should **assess the potential client,** to see whether they want to be engaged by them. Some firms will use checklists of standard questions to come to this conclusion.

Factors for consideration in client screening

- Management integrity
- Risk
- Relationships
- Ability to perform the work
- Engagement economics

High risk	Low risk
Poor performance	Good prospects
Lack of finance	Well-financed
Odd accounting	Strong controls
Lack of FD	Prudent accounting
Significant related party/ unusual transactions	Competent directors
	No unusual transactions

Sources of information about new clients

1. Enquiries of other sources (bankers, solicitors)
2. Review of documents (most recent annual accounts, listing particulars, credit rating)
3. Previous auditors (previous auditors should disclose fully all relevant information)
4. Review of rules/standards (consider specific laws/standards that relate to industry)

The **audit engagement letter** is the written terms of an engagement in the form of a letter.

Guidance on engagement letters is given in ISA 210 *Agreeing the Terms of Audit Engagements*. It applies to audit assignments **only**.

ISA 210

The auditor must first establish whether the preconditions for an audit are present. (ISA 210: para. 6)

The auditor must also confirm there is a common understanding between the auditor and the client on the terms of the engagement. (ISA 210: para. 9)

The audit engagement letter

- Objective and scope of the audit
- Auditor's responsibilities
- Management's responsibilities
- Identification of applicable financial reporting framework
- Expected form and content of any reports (ISA 210: para. 10)

Additional matters that can be included (ISA 210: para. A23)

- Elaboration of scope
- Form of any other communication
- Unavoidable risk of not detecting some material misstatements
- Planning and performance arrangements
- Expectation of provision of written representations
- Agreement to provide draft financial statements
- Agreement to inform auditor of facts that may affect financial statements
- Fees and billing
- Request to acknowledge receipt of letter and to agree terms
- Involvement of other auditors, experts
- Involvement of internal auditors, other staff
- Predecessor auditor
- Restriction of auditor's liability
- Any further agreements
- Obligations to provide audit working papers to other parties

The ultimate responsibility for audit quality rests with the engagement partner.

Guidance on quality control over individual audit engagements is given in ISA 220 *Quality Control for an Audit of Financial Statements*.

- Leadership responsibilities
- Ethical requirement
- Acceptance/continuance
- Assignment of engagement teams
- Engagement performance — Direction; Supervision; Review; Consultation; Resolving disputes
- Engagement quality control review — For audits of listed entries for other entities which meet firm's review criteria
- Monitoring

5: Internal audit

Topic List

Internal audit is an important control function in an organisation and an example of good corporate governance. This chapter looks at the best practice recommendations of the UK Corporate Governance Code in relation to the internal audit function, as well as contrasting the rules of internal and external audit.

We also look at the types of assignment carried out by internal audit, reporting and the advantages and disadvantages of outsourcing the internal audit function.

Internal audit is likely to be examined in a scenario question, perhaps in conjunction with corporate governance.

Internal audit is a function of an entity that performs assurance and consulting activities designed to evaluate and improve the effectiveness of the entity's governance, risk management and internal control process. (IFAC, 2016)

Internal audit and the audit committee

The **UK Corporate Governance Code**, as an example of an international code on corporate governance, recommends that the audit committee of a company should:

- Monitor and review effectiveness of internal audit activities.
- If there is no internal audit function, consider annually whether there is need for one.
- If there is no internal audit function, explain this absence in the annual report.

(FRC UK Corporate Governance Code: s. C.3.1–C.3.8)

Distinction between internal and external audit

	Purpose	Scope	Relationship to company	Reporting	Fraud
Internal audit	An activity designed to add value and improve an organisations operations	Internal audit's work relates to the operations of the organisation	Internal auditors are often employees of the organisation, although sometimes the internal audit function is outsourced.	Internal audit reports to senior management and audit committee	Prevention and detection of fraud is management's responsibility. But internal auditors should be alert to risks and exposures that could allow fraud.
External audit	An exercise to enable auditors to express an opinion on the financial statements	External audit's work relates to the financial statements. They are concerned with the financial records that underlie these.	External auditors are independent of the company and its management. They are appointed by the shareholders.	Auditor's report addressed to shareholders	Prevention and detection of fraud is management's responsibility.

'**Value for money**' is a performance measure summarised in three qualities (which a product or activity possesses):

- **Economy**
- **Efficiency**
- **Effectiveness**

Management should, as part of normal business process, assess economy, efficiency and effectiveness in operations (a value for money audit).

Value for money audit is an assignment which internal audit can undertake on behalf of management in its **monitoring** role.

It can be carried out on any area of the business at the request of management (eg service delivery, management process, environment).

Economy: Attaining the appropriate quantity and quality of physical, human and financial resources (inputs) at the lowest cost.

Efficiency: This is a measure of the relationship between goods and services produced (outputs) and the resources used to produce them (inputs).

Effectiveness: How well an activity is achieving its policy objectives or other intended effects.

Financial audits are more the traditional realm of the internal auditors. These involve reviewing the company records and other available evidence to substantiate information in financial and management reporting.

'**Best value**' is a performance framework introduced in local authorities by the UK government, whereby they should implement the 4 'Cs':

- **Challenge** (how and why is a service provided?)
- **Compare** (to other authorities/private sector)
- **Consult** (targets set in consultation with tax payers/service users)
- **Compete** (fair competition)

Internal audit can **monitor best value** to ensure that the authority has systems in place to achieve best value. Internal audit will also be involved in **setting up best value** because a good understanding of current systems is needed.

Information technology audits

Information technology is an increasingly important area of business. Internal audit can monitor and test controls in the following areas:

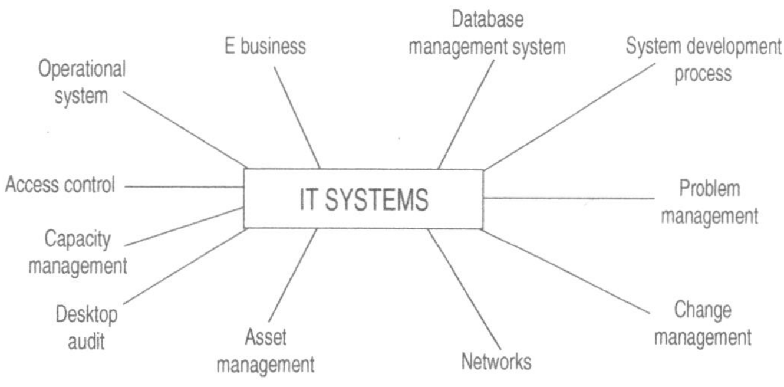

Operational audits are audits of the operational processes of the organisation. They are also known as management, or efficiency audits. Their prime objective is monitoring of management's performance, ensuring company policy is adhered to.

Approaching operational audit assignments

There are two aspects of an operational assignment:

- Ensure policies are adequate
- Ensure policies work effectively

Procurement audits

- Focus on systems in the purchases department
- Objectives and tests as are outlined in Chapter 10 where the purchases system will be discussed

Other assignments

- Testing controls
- Fraud investigations
- Customer service reviews
- Review of compliance with laws

Procedures

1. Obtain **written copies of the policies** in the area to be audited.
2. **Read** them and **assess** whether they are adequate to meet objectives.
3. **Discuss** the policies with members of the department to ensure understanding is correct.
4. Examine the **effectiveness** of controls by **observing** them in operation and testing them (by similar methods to those considered in Chapters 9–10).
5. **Report to management** on adequacy and effectiveness, giving suggestions for improvement in both areas where required.

Internal audit reports

There are two types of internal audit report:

- **Risk-based**
- **Performance enhancement**

Most work is likely to be risk-based but either way, a formal report will be the result.

There is usually no formal requirement for internal audit reports, however the generally accepted report format for business includes the following:

- Terms of reference
- Executive summary
- Body of report
- Appendices for additional information

Draft report – discussed at an **exit meeting**.

Contents of executive summary

- Background to assignment
- Objectives
- Major outcomes
- Key risks identified
- Key action points
- Summary of work left to do

Report should describe **purpose, scope** and **results** of the engagement.

Internal audit reports should be dated, marked as 'draft' or 'final' and include a distribution list.

Outsourcing is the process of purchasing key functions from an outside source. Audit firms (particularly larger ones) are increasingly offering internal audit services as part of their portfolio.

Outsourcing

Outsourcing

- Service provider has good quality staff
- Ensures team with specialist skill/qualifications
- Provides immediate team
- Can be appointed for appropriate timescale
- Is likely to cost less than setting up a department

Not outsourcing

- Cost of recruiting staff (to the service provider)
- Need for staff of particular skill/qualification
- Difficulty of managing an IA department for directors
- Extended time frame between set up and results
- Work involved may not justify a full-time team
- Team might be required due to variety of skills needed

Managing an outsourced department

The company will need to establish **controls** to manage the outsourced internal audit function.

Controls over outsourced internal audit function

- Performance measures for cost and areas reviewed
- Maintenance of appropriate audit methodology
- Review of working papers on a sample basis
- Agreement of work plans in advance
- If external auditor from same firm, ensure firm has safeguards to keep the functions separate to maintain independence and objectivity

6: Risk assessment

Topic List

Risk

Materiality

Understanding the entity

Assessing risk

Fraud, law and regulations

Documentation of risk assessment

This chapter examines audit risk, materiality and the use of analytical procedures at the audit planning stage.

Risk assessment is a key topic area and may come up in a scenario-based question where you are asked to identify risks from the information provided to you in the question and explain why they are risks.

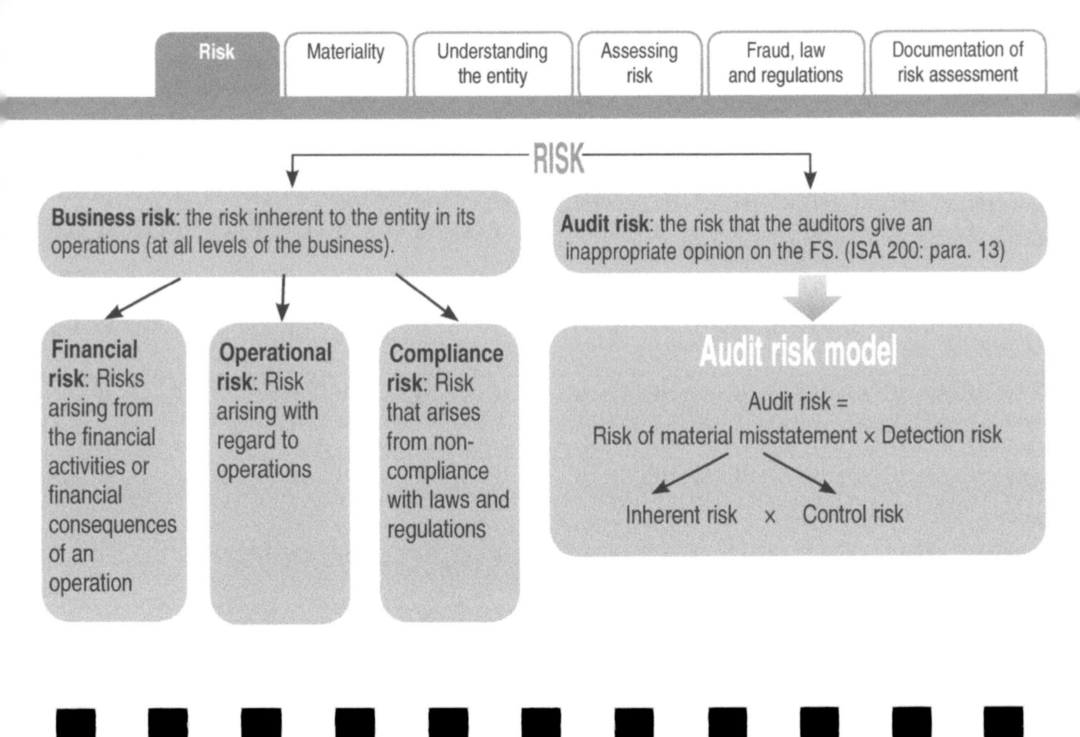
RISK
Business risk: the risk inherent to the entity in its operations (at all levels of the business).
Financial risk: Risks arising from the financial activities or financial consequences of an operation
Operational risk: Risk arising with regard to operations
Compliance risk: Risk that arises from non-compliance with laws and regulations
Audit risk: the risk that the auditors give an inappropriate opinion on the FS. (ISA 200: para. 13)
Audit risk model
Audit risk =
Risk of material misstatement × Detection risk
Inherent risk × Control risk

The components of audit risk (ISA 200: para. 13)

Inherent risk is the susceptibility of an assertion to a misstatement that could be material, individually or when aggregated with other misstatements, before consideration of any related internal controls.

Control risk is the risk that a material misstatement that could occur in an assertion and that could be material, individually or when aggregated with other misstatements, will not be prevented or detected and corrected on a timely basis by the entity's internal control.

Detection risk is the risk that the auditor's procedures will not detect a misstatement that exists in an assertion that could be material, individually or when aggregated with other misstatements.

ISA 200 *Overall Objectives of the Independent Auditor and the Conduct of an Audit in Accordance with International Standards on Auditing* states that auditors must plan and perform the audit with an attitude of **professional scepticism** (ISA 200: para. 15).

Materiality

Guidance on materiality for the financial statements as a whole, and on performance materiality is given in ISA 320 *Materiality in Planning and Performing an Audit*.

Information is **material** if its omission or misstatement could influence the economic decisions of users taken on the basis of the financial statements. (ISA 200: para. 6)

Performance materiality is the amount(s) set by the auditor at less than materiality for the financial statements as a whole, to reduce to an appropriately low level the probability that the aggregate of uncorrected and undetected misstatements exceeds materiality for the financial statements as a whole.

Performance materiality also refers to the amount(s) set by the auditor at less than materiality for particular classes of transactions, account balances or disclosures. (ISA 320: para. 9)

To calculate a level of materiality for the financial statements as a whole, the auditor will often use the benchmarks below, although professional judgement must be applied:

Calculating materiality

- **Profit before tax**: 5%
- **Gross profit**: 0.5 – 1%
- **Revenue**: 0.5 – 1%
- **Total assets**: 1 – 2%
- **Net assets**: 2 – 5%
- **Profit after tax**: 5 – 10%

ISA 315 *Identifying and Assessing the Risks of Material Misstatement through Understanding the Entity and its Environment* provides guidance.

Risk assessment

The auditor shall perform a risk assessment to provide a basis for the identification and assessment of risks of material misstatement. (ISA 315: para. 5)

The engagement team shall discuss the susceptibility of the entity's financial statements to material misstatements and the application of the applicable financial reporting framework to the entity's facts and circumstances. (ISA 315: para. 10)

Risk assessment procedures shall include:

- **Inquiries** of management/internal auditors/ others in entity
- **Analytical procedures**
- **Observation** and **inspection**

The auditor may also perform other procedures where circumstances merit it.

(ISA 315: para. 6)

Matters to gain understanding of (from ISA 315 paras. 11–12)

- Relevant industry, regulatory and other external factors including applicable reporting framework
- Nature of the entity
- Selection, application and suitability of accounting policies
- Entity's objectives and strategies and related business risks that could lead to material misstatement
- Measurement and review of the entity's financial performance
- Internal control relevant to the audit:
  - Control environment
  - Entity's risk assessment process
  - Information system relevant to financial reporting
  - Entity's communication of financial reporting matters
  - Control activities relevant to the audit
  - Activities to monitor internal control over financial reporting

Assessing risk

ISA 330 *The Auditor's Responses to Assessed Risks* requires the auditor to obtain sufficient appropriate audit evidence regarding assessed risks by designing and implementing appropriate responses. (ISA 330: para. 3)

Reducing risk

To reduce audit risk to an acceptably low level, the auditor shall determine overall responses to the assessed risks at the financial statement level and shall design and perform further audit procedures to respond to assessed risks at the assertion level.

(ISA 330: paras. 5 & 6)

Financial statement level possible responses

- Emphasise professional scepticism to team
- Assign more experienced staff
- Provide more supervision
- Incorporate more unpredictability into testing
- Make general changes to nature, timing or extent of audit procedures

Assertion level possible responses

Design and perform audit procedures whose nature, timing and extent are responsive to the assessed risks of material misstatement, eg tests of controls only, substantive procedures only, a combined approach.

Fraud

This includes:

- Fraudulent financial reporting
- Misappropriation of assets

(ISA 240: para. 3)

Responsibilities

Management and those charged with governance are responsible for prevention and detection.

Auditors must be aware of the possibility of misstatement due to fraud. (ISA 240: paras. 4 & 5)

Under ISA 240

The auditor shall identify and assess the risks of material misstatements in the financial statements due to fraud, both at the financial statement level and at the assertion level.

Risk assessment procedures

- Inquiries of management/those charged with governance
- Consideration of fraud risk factors (these are listed in an appendix to ISA 240)
- Consideration of results of analytical procedures
- Consideration of other relevant information

Law and regulations

Under ISA 250

The auditor shall obtain a general understanding of the legal and regulatory framework applicable to the entity and how the entity is complying with that framework.

Reporting

Fraud

- To the **appropriate level of management** if auditor has identified/is suspicious of fraud
- To **those charged with governance** if fraud involves management or significant employees
- To **regulators** if there is a statutory duty
- In **auditor's report** if necessary

Law and regulations

- To **those charged with governance** or obtain evidence that they are appropriately informed
- To **audit committee**/supervisory board if senior management implicated
- To **regulators** if there is a statutory duty
- In **auditor's report**: if non-compliance has a material effect and has not been properly reflected

Auditors should bear in mind their professional duty of confidentiality and seek legal advice, if required.

ISAs 315 (para. 32) and 330 (paras. 28–32) require **documentation** at the risk assessment stage of the audit.

Matters to be documented

- Discussion among audit team
- Understanding of the entity and its controls
- Identified and assessed risks of material misstatement
- Risks identified and related controls evaluated
- Overall responses
- Nature, extent and timing of further audit procedures
- Results of audit procedures
- If relying on evidence on controls from prior audit, conclusions regarding appropriateness
- Demonstration that the financial statements agree or reconcile with underlying accounting records

7: Audit planning and documentation

Topic List

Planning is a vital stage of the audit process and is linked to risk assessment which was introduced in the previous chapter.

The importance of maintaining and retaining audit documentation is also considered here.

This topic could come up in a scenario question asking you to identify audit risks or in a knowledge-based question on the audit strategy or audit plan.

ISA 300 *Planning an Audit of Financial Statements* (para. 2) sets out the objectives of planning:

1. To help the auditor to devote appropriate attention to important areas
2. To help identify and resolve potential problems on a timely basis
3. To perform the audit in an effective manner
4. To assist in selecting appropriate team members and in assignment of work
5. To facilitate the direction, supervision and review of work
6. To assist in co-ordination of work done by auditors of components and experts

The **audit strategy** sets the scope, timing and direction of the audit, and guides the development of the detailed audit plan. (ISA 300: para. 7)

The **audit plan** converts the audit strategy into a more detailed plan and includes the nature, timing and extent of audit procedures in order to obtain sufficient appropriate audit evidence to reduce audit risk to an acceptably low level. (ISA 300: para. 9)

Audit strategy: matters to consider (ISA 300: para. 8)

- Characteristics of the engagement
- Reporting objectives, timing of audit and nature of communications
- Significant factors, preliminary engagement activities, and knowledge gained on other engagements
- Nature, timing and extent of resources

The audit plan must include the following:

1. Nature, timing and extent of planned risk assessment procedures
2. Nature, timing and extent of further audit procedures at assertion level
3. Any other planned audit procedures required to comply with ISAs

The audit strategy and audit plan shall be updated and changed as necessary during the course of the audit, with any changes, and reasons for them, documented. (ISA 300: para. 12)

Auditors may plan to carry out the audit in two sittings – an **interim audit** and a **final audit**. The interim audit occurs during the period of review and focuses on risk assessment/internal control evaluation. The final audit focuses on the financial statements.

Audit documentation is the record of audit procedures performed, relevant audit evidence obtained and conclusions the auditor reached (also called 'working papers'). (ISA 230: para. 6)

Guidance is given in ISA 230 *Audit Documentation*.

Objectives of audit documentation (ISA 230: para. 3)

- Provides evidence of auditor's basis for conclusion
- Provides evidence that audit was planned and performed in accordance with ISAs
- Assists engagement team to plan and perform audit
- Assists in direction, supervision and review of audit work
- Enables team to be accountable
- Allows a record of matters of continuing significance to be retained
- Enables conduct of quality control reviews and inspections

Factors affecting form and content of documentation (ISA 230: A2)

- Size and complexity of entity
- Nature of audit procedures
- Identified risks
- Significance of evidence obtained
- Nature and extent of exceptions
- Need to document a conclusion
- Audit methodology and tools used

Audit documentation will be split between **current audit files** and **permanent audit files**.

Current audit files contain information relevant to current year (eg financial statements, review notes, audit plan, management letter).

Permanent audit files contain information of continuing importance (eg engagement letter, legal documents, board minutes, prior years' financial statements).

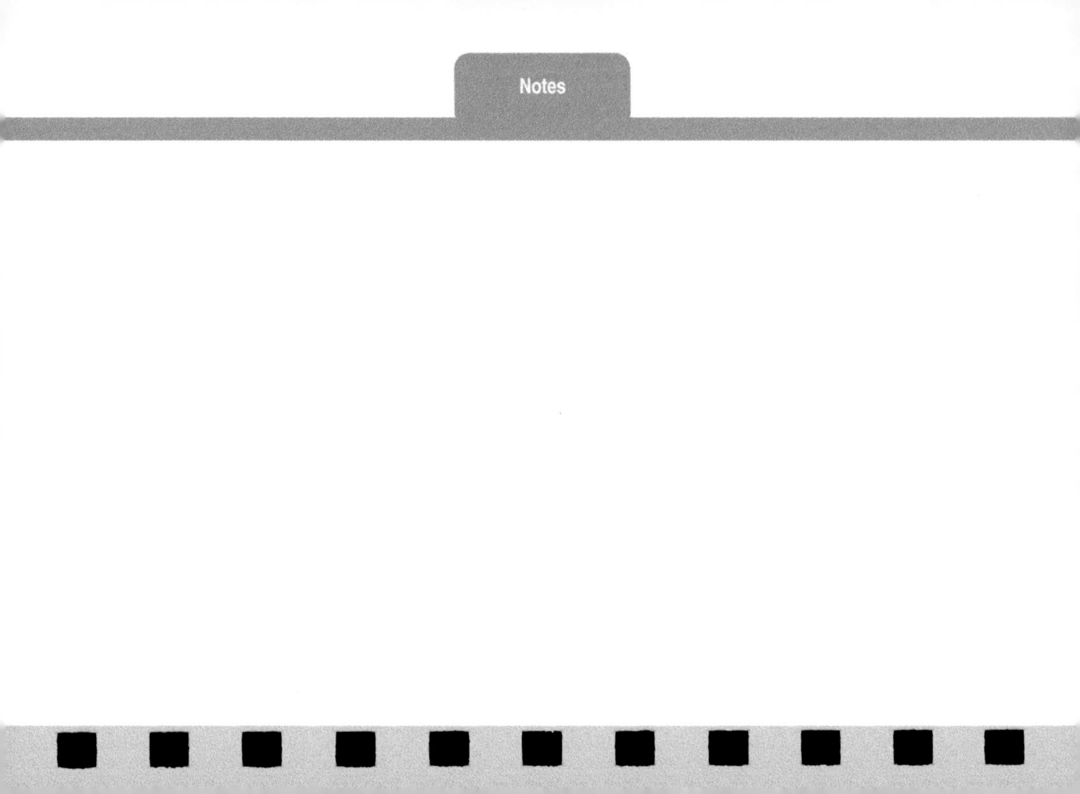
Notes

8: Introduction to audit evidence

Topic List

The auditor obtains evidence in order to form the audit opinion. It is vital that this evidence is:

- *Sufficient*
- *Appropriate*

This chapter describes the financial statement assertions over which audit evidence is required. These are very important as exam questions will tend to focus on audit procedures required to test particular assertions.

Audit evidence is all of the information used by the auditor in arriving at the conclusions on which the audit opinion is based. (ISA 500: para. 5)

ISA 500 *Audit Evidence* gives guidance:

Under ISA 500

Auditors must design and perform audit procedures to obtain **sufficient appropriate** audit evidence. (ISA 500: para. 6)

Sufficiency (ISA 500: para. A4)

Quantity

Influenced by:

- Risk assessment
- Nature of systems
- Materiality of item
- Experience
- Source and reliability
- Results of procedures

Appropriateness (ISA 500: para. A5)

Quality

External evidence (more reliable than internal)
Auditor evidence (collected from auditors better than obtained from entity)
Entity evidence (more reliable when controls effective)
Written evidence (more reliable than oral)
Original evidence (original better than photocopies)

Financial statement assertions are the representations by management, explicit or otherwise, that are embodied in the financial statements, as used by the auditor to consider the different types of potential misstatements that may occur. (ISA 315: para. 4)

Assertions (ISA 315: para. A124)

- About classes of transactions and events and related disclosures (occurrence, completeness, accuracy, cut-off, classification and presentation)
- About account balances and related disclosures at the period end (existence, rights and obligations, accuracy, valuation and allocation, classification and presentation)

Audit procedures

These are carried out to:

- Obtain an understanding of the entity and its environment to assess risks (**risk assessment procedures**).
- Test operating effectiveness of controls (**tests of controls**).
- Detect misstatements (**substantive procedures**).

Audit procedures (ISA 500: paras. A14-A25)

- Inspection of tangible assets
- Inspection of documentation or records
- Observation
- Inquiry
- Confirmation
- Recalculation
- Reperformance
- Analytical procedures

9: Internal control

Topic List

Internal controls are a key topic area and this chapter is essential background to Chapter 10 which looks at practical aspects of controls testing in the context of the key transactions cycles.

Internal control is the process designed, implemented and maintained by those charged with governance, management and other personnel, to provide reasonable assurance about the achievement of the entity's objectives with regard to reliability of financial reporting, effectiveness and efficiency of operations and compliance with applicable laws and regulations. (ISA 315: para. 4)

Components of internal control (ISA 315: paras. 14–24)

- Control environment
- Risk assessment process
- The information system relevant to financial reporting
- Control activities
- Monitoring of controls

Relevant controls

Not all controls are relevant to the auditor's risk assessment. The auditor is primarily concerned with those which are part of the management of risk that may give rise to a material misstatement in the FS.

Control environment (ISA 315: para. A77)

The attitudes, awareness and actions of management.

- Communication and enforcement of integrity and ethical values
- Commitment to competence
- Participation by those charged with governance
- Management's philosophy and operating style
- Organisational structure
- Assignment of authority and responsibility
- Human resource policies and practices

Risk assessment process (ISA 315: para. 15)

The process of identifying and responding to business risk.

Risk can arise due to:

- Changes in operating environment
- New personnel
- New/revamped information systems
- Rapid growth
- New technology
- New business models, products or activities
- Corporate restructuring
- Expanded foreign operations
- New accounting pronouncements

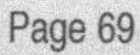

Information system (ISA 315: para. A89)

This consists of:

- Infrastructure (physical/hardware)
- Software
- People
- Procedures
- Data

The IS relevant to FR objectives **initiates, records, processes** and **reports** transactions.

+

Control activities (ISA 315: para. A96)

Policies and procedures which ensure that management directives are carried out.

- Performance reviews
- Information processing
- Physical controls
- Segregation of duties

Monitoring of controls (ISA 315: para. A106)

A process to assess the quality of internal control performance over time:

- Operating as intended/modified as appropriate
- Internal audit may perform part of this function

Limitations of internal control (ISA 315: paras. A53–A55)

Exam focus

Internal control only provides directors with **reasonable assurance** that objectives are met because internal control has inherent limitations.

- **Costs** of control outweigh the benefit

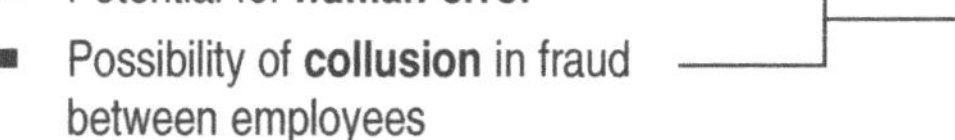

- Potential for **human error**
- Possibility of **collusion** in fraud between employees

  → Hence segregation of duties is vital

- Controls could be bypassed/ **overridden** by management
- Controls are designed to cope with routine transactions not **non-routine** ones

Auditors must record the client's systems. Narrative notes, flowcharts questionnaires or checklists may be used.

Narrative notes

- **Advantage:** Easy to record
- **Disadvantage:** Difficult to update (unless computerised)

Aim to describe and explain the system.
Can support flowcharts.

Flowcharts

- **Advantages**: Quick to prepare, easy to follow, complete system, eliminate extensive narrative
- **Disadvantages:** Only suitable for standard systems, good for document flow not controls, difficult to amend, can waste time

Questionnaires

Two main types:

- Internal control questionnaire (ICQ)
- Internal control evaluation questionnaire (ICEQ)

ICQs Try to answer the question 'are the desirable controls present?'

ICEQs Try to establish if specific frauds/errors are possible.

The advantages of questionnaires are that they are thorough and quick.

Checklists

Similar to internal control questionnaire.

Assessing internal controls

Assessment of systems

Auditors:

- **Assess the adequacy** of the accounting systems as the basis for the FS
- **Identify** the types of **potential misstatement** that could occur in the FS
- Consider **factors** that affect the risk of misstatements
- **Design appropriate audit procedures**

The auditors must gain an understanding of the information system so that they can understand the **major classes of transaction**, **how** transactions are **initiated**, what the **significant records** are, and what the **financial reporting process** is.

Risk assessment procedures

To obtain an understanding of the entity and its environment:

- Inquiries of management and other personnel
- Analytical procedures
- Observation and inspection

ie assessment of controls is an integral part of risk assessment (see Chapter 6).

Assessment of control risk

Auditors shall carry out tests of controls if:

- Risk assessment indicated that controls are operating effectively.
- The auditor has determined it is not possible/ practicable to reduce risk at assertion level to acceptable level by substantive procedures.

(ISA 330: para. 8)

Tests of controls

Tests of controls are performed to obtain audit evidence about the operating effectiveness of controls in **preventing**, or **detecting** and **correcting** material misstatements. (ISA 330: para. 4)

Tests of controls may include:

- **Inquiries** about and **observation** of control procedures
- **Inspection** of documents supporting controls
- **Examination of evidence of management views**
- **Reperformance** of control procedures to ensure they were correctly performed
- **Testing** on controls operating on specific **computer applications**

If risk assessment has shown controls to be ineffective testing will not be undertaken. It may also be **inefficient** to test controls if the population consists of a few large items which can be tested quickly by substantive tests.

When controls testing is completed, auditors make a final assessment of control risk, and **revise** the nature, timing and extent of **substantive procedures** accordingly.

Auditors should consider: **how** controls were applied, **how consistently** they were applied and **by whom** (ISA 330: para. 10). Controls testing is often completed on an **interim audit**.

Auditors should **combine** inquiry with another type of procedure when testing controls. (ISA 330. A26)

In a computerised environment, there are two important types of control.

General controls are controls required over development (systems design and testing), changes to programs (passwords/records of changes maintained), testing of program changes, prevention of incorrect use (operation controls) and controls to ensure continuity (back-up and disaster recovery). (IFAC, 2016)

Application controls relate to procedures used to initiate, record, process and report transactions. (IFAC, 2016)

It is important that management have an IT security and use policy which should include the following:

- Procedures including passwords, data protection and information distribution
- Legal requirements (data protection legislation) and licensing agreements
- Commitment to information security
- Overall supervision by senior management
- Consequence of disobeying the rules

Notes

10: Tests of controls

Topic List

It is important to be comfortable with:

- *Examples of controls for specific transaction areas*
- *What the control is trying to achieve (objective)*

Some examples of tests of controls have been given in the shaded boxes in this chapter. However, they are not exhaustive. Remember that the test is seeking to establish whether the control is effective. If you bear that in mind you should be able to tailor tests of controls to the specific scenario in the question. You will also need to be able to explain why you would carry out a particular test of controls.

Aims of control

Ordering/granting credit

- Sale made to good credit ratings
- Who are encouraged to pay promptly
- Orders are correct
- Orders are fulfilled

Dispatch/invoicing

- All despatches are recorded
- Invoicing is correct and for goods supplied
- Credit notes given are for valid reasons

Accounting/recording/credit control

- Transactions are recorded
- In correct accounts
- In correct period
- Irrecoverable debts identified

Controls

Ordering/granting credit

- Segregation of duties (credit control/invoice/despatch)
- Authorisation of credit terms (checks obtained review)
- Sequential numbering of pre-printed order forms
- Correct prices quoted to customers
- Match orders to dispatch notes (o/s orders queried)
- Dealing with customer queries

Dispatch/invoicing

- Authorisation of dispatch
- Examination of goods despatched (quality)
- Recording of goods outward
- Match dispatch notes to order/invoice (o/s queried)
- Sequential numbering of pre-printed dispatch notes
- Signature of customer on delivery notes
- Authorisation of price on invoice (price list)
- Arithmetical checks on invoices

Accounting/recording/credit control

- Segregation of duties (recording sales/statements)
- Recording of sequence of sales invoices
- Matching cash receipts with invoices
- Retention of customer remittance advices
- Preparation/checking of receivables' statements
- Review/chase overdue accounts/authorised write-off
- Reconciliation of receivables ledger control account

Tests of controls

Test for evidence of:

- References
- Authorisation
- Credit terms/limits
- Matching orders

Verify matching of sales invoices with dispatch notes.

Test numerical sequences of records (enquire about gaps).

Observe quality inspections or inspect documentary evidence of inspections.

Review invoices for evidence arithmetical checks have occurred.

Review entries in ledger, scrutinise for credit limits, inspect reconciliations.

Aims of control

Ordering

- Orders are authorised and for the company
- Made from authorised suppliers
- At good prices

Receipt/invoice

- Only accepted if from authorised order
- Accurately recorded
- Liabilities recognised for goods received
- Credits are claimed

Accounting

- Expenditure is only for received goods
- Authorised
- Properly recorded
- In correct account
- In correct period

Controls

Ordering

- Segregation of duties (requisitioning/ordering)
- Central policy for choice of supplier
- Use of pre-numbered purchase requisitions
- Authorised, pre-numbered (safeguarded) order forms
- Monitoring of supplier terms for most favourable

Goods received

- Examine goods inwards (quality) and record deliveries
- Compare goods received notes (GRNs) with orders
- Reference suppliers' invoices
- Check suppliers' invoices (maths, prices, quantities)
- Record goods returns
- Have procedures for obtaining credit notes

Accounting

- Segregation of duties (recording/checking)
- Prompt recording in day books and ledgers
- Comparison of supplier statements to ledger accounts
- Authorisation of payments (limits/goods received)
- Review of allocation of expenditure
- Reconciliation of payables ledger with total of balances
- Procedures for cut-off

Tests of controls

It is important that auditors test that invoices are supported by genuine purchase orders, authorised by correct individual. Inspect invoices to ensure they are supported by GRNs, authorised, priced correctly, coded correctly, entered in inventory, maths correct, posted to ledger.

Review numerical sequences.

Observe whether the purchase day book is referenced to invoices.

Review a sample of supplier statement reconciliations.

Inspect control account reconciliations.

Aims of controls

Recording

- All inventory movements recorded/authorised
- All inventories recorded are owned by company
- Inventories recorded exist
- Inventory quantities recorded are correct
- Cut-off procedures correctly applied

Protection

- Safeguarded against loss/theft/damage

Valuation

- Costing system values inventories correctly
- Allowance made for slow moving/obsolete inventories

Inventory holding

- Levels of inventories held are reasonable

Controls

Recording

- Segregation of duties (custody/recording)
- Goods inwards met and checked
- Inventory issues supported by documentation
- Inventory records maintained

Protection

- Precautions against theft (restriction)
- Precautions against deterioration
- Security over inventory held by third parties
- Regular inventory taking

Valuation

- Valuation agrees with IAS 2 *Inventories*
- Calculations are checked
- Condition of inventories is reviewed
- Accounting for waste is provided for

Inventory holding

- Provision made for inventory levels
- Minimum/maximum inventory levels exist

Tests of controls

Observe and test check inventory counts, ensure discrepancies are investigated, authorised and corrected.

Review inventory count instructions and ensure staff have been provided with a copy.

Inventory counting is covered in more detail in Chapter 13.

Observe goods inwards inspection.

Check sequence of inventory records.

Observe security arrangements for inventories.

Consider the environment in which inventories are held.

Cash system: aims of controls

- All monies received are banked, recorded and safeguarded against loss/theft.
- All payments are authorised, made out to the correct payees, recorded.
- Payments are not made twice for the same liability.

Controls

Receipts

- Segregation of duties
- Post stamped with date of receipt
- Restrictions on receipt of cash (salespeople only)
- Agreement of cash collections to till rolls
- Prompt maintenance of records
- Giving and recording receipts for cash

Bank

- Daily bankings, banking of receipts intact
- Restrictions on opening new bank accounts
- Limitations on cash floats
- Surprise cash counts
- Custody of cash and cheques
- Restrictions on issuing blank cheques
- Bank reconciliations

Payments

- Cheque requisitions supported by documentation/authorised
- Authorised signatories
- Prompt dispatch of signed cheques
- Payments recorded promptly
- Cash payments authorised
- Limit on disbursements
- Rules of cash advances to employees

Tests of controls

Observe 'post opening'. Trace entries on listing to cash book, paying in book, bank statement.

Observe whether cash is banked daily.

Review records for evidence that cash receipts are agreed to till rolls (eg signatures, spreadsheet entries).

Review documentation for evidence of agreement of cash receipts from cash book to paying-in slips, bank, posting to the sales ledger, posting to the general ledger.

For cash payments, check that cheques are signed by authorised signatories (paid cheques can be requested from the bank), check to supplier invoice, verify that supporting documents are stamped 'paid'. Review postings to the ledgers.

Review a sample of bank reconciliations to ensure properly carried out.

Observe a cash count.

Payroll system: aims of controls

- Employees only paid authorised amounts for work done
- Deductions are recorded and pay agrees to bank records
- Correct employees are paid
- Deductions are correct and paid over to the correct authorities

Controls

- Segregation of duties
- Authorisation of changes and payments
- Password protection for computerised payroll
- Custody of cash for cash payouts
- Maintenance of salary bank account
- Reconciliation of accounts
- Reconciliation of wages costs to payroll records
- Reconciliations of deductions
- Surprise cash counts

Tests of controls

It is vital to check that all aspects of the payroll (amounts/deductions/payments) are authorised.

Attend cash payouts to ensure controlled.

Test password protection by inputting test data. Review reconciliations to ensure properly carried out and that discrepancies are followed up.

Capital and revenue expenditure: aims of controls

- **Authorisation**

  All expenditure is authorised (see purchases above).
- **Recording**

  All expenditure is correctly classified in the FS as capital or revenue expenditure.

Tests of controls

It is vital that auditors check that all invoices are supported by genuine purchase orders, authorised by the correct individual.

Controls

Ordering

- Orders for capital items should be authorised specifically
- Should be requisitioned on different documentation

Invoices

- Should be approved by authorised person
- Should be coded correctly

Recording

- Capital items should be written in the non-current asset register
- Non-current asset register reconciled to general ledger
- Segregation of duties (requisitioning/ordering)
- Central policy for choice of supplier

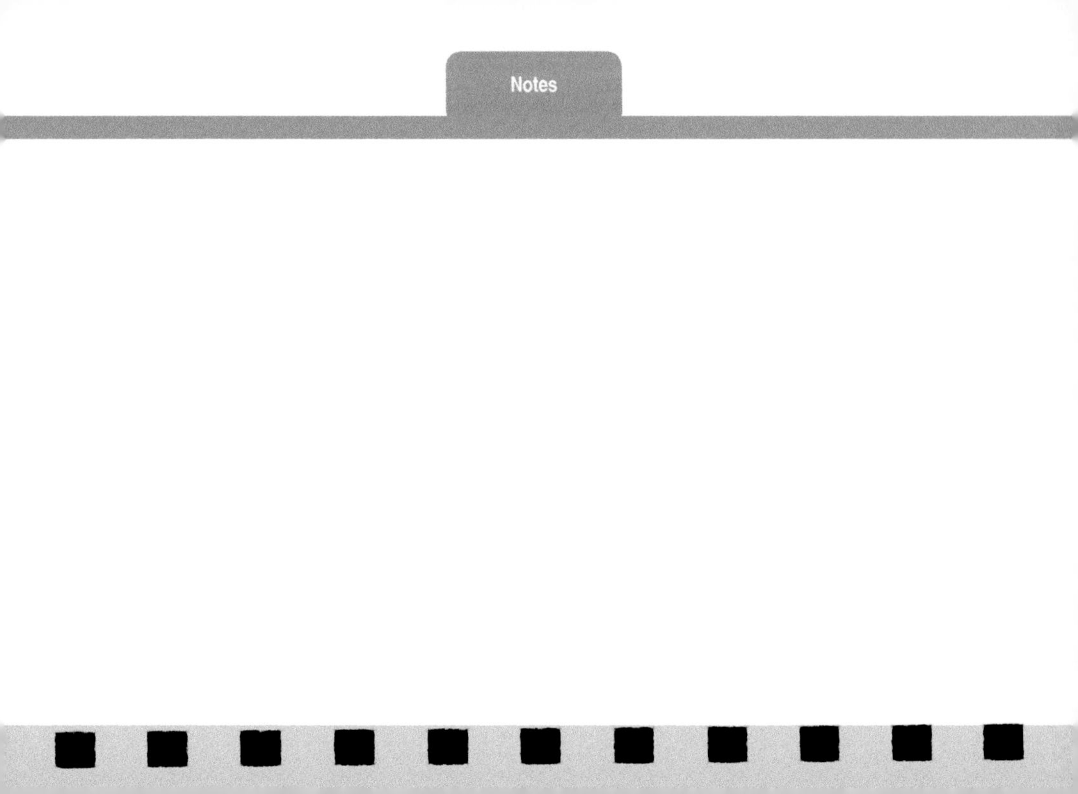

Notes

11: Audit procedures and sampling

Topic List

In this chapter, we look at substantive procedures, including analytical procedures.

We also look at the audit of accounting estimates, and the use of sampling and CAATs when carrying out audit procedures.

Auditors can often rely on the work of others such as experts and internal auditors during the audit and this is also considered in this chapter.

The topics in this chapter are likely to come up in the exam frequently, either in a scenario or a knowledge-based question.

Auditors need to obtain sufficient appropriate audit evidence to support the financial statement assertions. This is done through **substantive testing**.

Substantive procedures are tests to detect material misstatements in the FS. They are generally of two types:

- Analytical procedures
- Other procedures

(ISA 330: para. 4)

Model for an audit plan:

- Agree opening balances to last year's working papers
- Review general ledger for unusual records
- Check client schedule to/from accounting records/FS
- Carry out analytical review
- Test transactions in detail
- Test balances in detail
- Review presentation and disclosure in the FS

Directional testing

Substantive tests fall into **two categories** (broadly speaking).

- Tests to discover **errors** start **in** the accounting records.
- Tests to discover **omissions** start **outside** of the accounting records.

Test item

Test **debit items** (expenditure or assets) for overstatement by selecting debit entries recorded in the general ledger and checking value, existence and ownership.

Test **credit items** (income or liabilities) for understatement by selecting items from appropriate sources independent of the general ledger and ensuring that there is a correct general ledger entry.

Example

If a non-current asset entry in the general ledger of $1,000 is selected, it would be overstated if it should have been recorded at anything less than $1,000 or if the company did not own it, or indeed if it did not exist.

Select a goods despatched note and check that the resultant sale has been recorded in the general ledger sales account. Sales would be understated if the nominal ledger did not reflect the transaction at all (completeness) or reflected it at less than full value.

Exam focus

A test for the overstatement of an asset simultaneously gives comfort on understatement of other assets, overstatement of liabilities, overstatement of income and understatement of expenses.

Analytical procedures are the evaluations of financial information through analysis of plausible relationships among both financial and non-financial data.

ISA 520 *Analytical Procedures* gives guidance on use of analytical procedures as substantive tests and overall review.

Analytical procedures (ISA 520: A1–A2)

(a) Comparisons of this year's financial information with:
   (i) Similar information for prior periods
   (ii) Anticipated results/budgets
   (iii) Industry information
   (iv) Expectations produced by the auditor

(b) Elements of financial information which are **expected to conform** to patterns

(c) **Links** between financial/non-financial information

Analytical procedures as substantive tests (ISA 520: para. 5)

- Determine **suitability** for given assertions
- Evaluate **reliability** of data
- Develop an **expectation** and evaluate whether **sufficiently precise**
- Determine amount of **acceptable difference**

Practical techniques

- Ratio analysis
- Examining related accounts
- Trend analysis
- Reasonableness tests

Significant fluctuations and unexpected relationships

When these are identified, the auditors shall:

- Make inquiries of directors.
- Consider management response in light of knowledge/evidence.
- Carry out other audit procedures where necessary.

(ISA 520: para. 7)

Auditors will use the primary **accounting ratios** (you should be familiar with these). There are also a number of significant relationships in FS:

Significant relationships

- Payables/purchases
- Inventories/cost of sales
- Non-current assets/depreciation/repairs expense
- Intangible assets/amortisation
- Loans/interest expense
- Investments/investment income
- Receivables/bad debt
- Expense/sales

An **accounting estimate** is an approximation of a monetary amount in the absence of a precise means of measurement, for example, allowances to reduce inventory/receivables to their estimated realisable value, depreciation, accrued revenue, provision for a lawsuit, construction contracts or warranty claims. (ISA 540: para. 7)

Guidance is given in ISA 540 *Auditing Accounting Estimates, Including Fair Value Accounting Estimates, and Related Disclosures.*

Audit procedures

- Consider reasonableness of assumptions
- Consider if management has considered alternative assumptions
- Evaluate whether estimates are reasonable or misstated
- Obtain evidence about accuracy of disclosures
- Evaluate adequacy of disclosure of estimation uncertainty for estimates that give rise to significant risks
- Consider if any management bias
- Obtain written representations whether management believes significant assumptions used are reasonable

Audit sampling is the application of audit procedures to less than 100% of items within a population of audit relevance such that all sampling units have a chance of selection. It uses either statistical sampling or non-statistical sampling methods. (ISA 530: para. 5)

Testing 100% of the population, and testing all items with a certain characteristic, are **not** audit sampling.

ISA 530 *Audit Sampling* provides guidance.

Design of sample-factors to consider (ISA 530: para. 6)

- Purpose of audit procedure
- Characteristics of population

Designing sample size

The auditor must design a sample size sufficient to reduce sampling risk to an acceptably low level. (ISA 530: para. 7)

Selection

- **Random** (all items have equal chance of selection)
- **Systematic** (constant interval between items)
- **Haphazard** (chosen at will, but guarding against bias in the selection)
- **Block** (check if items have particular characteristics)
- **Monetary unit sampling** (value-weighted selection)

Sampling risk arises from the possibility that the auditor's conclusion, based on a sample of a certain size, may be different from the conclusion that would be reached if the entire population were subjected to the same audit procedure. (ISA 530: para. 5)

Non-sampling risk arises from factors that cause the auditor to reach an erroneous conclusion for any reason not related to the size of the population (eg using inappropriate audit procedures). (ISA 530: para. 5)

Evaluation

Auditors must analyse any deviations or misstatements in the sample and draw inferences for the population as a whole. (ISA 530: para. 12)

Qualitative aspects of the error should be considered (nature of error/balance). Errors may be **projected** against the whole balance of the population.

Summary

- Determine objectives and characteristics of population
- Determine sample size
- Choose method of sample selection
- Project errors and evaluate results

IT brings many advantages to audit, particularly in areas such as analytical review.

CAATs are audit procedures performed using computers which can enhance the detail of the test undertaken and the result of the test. They consist of **audit software** and **test data**.

Audit software

This performs checks that auditors would otherwise have had to do by hand.

- **Interrogation** (data files)
- **Comparison** (comparing versions)
- **Interactive** (online)
- **Resident code** (as transactions are processed)

Test data

This is a way of **checking whether systems are operating properly;** feed the system some data to see how it is processed.

The data may be valid or invalid, depending on the objective of the test.

ISA 610 *Using the Work of Internal Auditors* provides guidance in this area.

The external auditor's objectives are:

1. To determine whether the work of internal auditors can be used, and if so, in which areas and to what extent.
2. To determine whether the work is adequate for the audit.

(ISA 610: para. 13)

If the auditors decide to make use of the work of internal audit, they must **evaluate** that work.

The important criteria when determining whether the work of the internal audit function can be used are:

- Extent to which its **objectivity** is supported
- Level of **competence**
- Whether approach is **systematic** and **disciplined**

(ISA 610: para. 15)

An **auditor's expert** is an individual or organisation possessing expertise in a field other than accounting or auditing, whose work in that field is used by the auditor to assist the auditor in obtaining sufficient appropriate audit evidence. (ISA 620: para. 6)

ISA 620 *Using the Work of an Auditor's Expert* requires the auditor to agree the following with the expert.

1. Nature, scope and objectives of their work
2. Respective roles and responsibilities
3. Nature, timing and extent of communication, including form of any report
4. Confidentiality requirements

A **service organisation** is a third-party organisation that provides services to user entites that are part of those entities' information systems relevant to financial reporting. (ISA 402: para. 8)

ISA 402 *Audit Considerations Relating to Entities Using Service Organisations* gives guidance:

- How the use of a service organisation affects the entity's internal control
- Nature and materiality of transactions processed
- Degree of interaction
- Nature of relationship

Under ISA 402

The auditor must obtain an understanding of the nature and significance of the services provided by the service organisation and their effect on the entity's internal control relevant to the audit, sufficient to identify and assess the risks of material misstatement and to design and perform relevant audit procedures to address those risks.
(ISA 402: para. 11)

12: Non-current assets

Topic List

This chapter looks at the audit of non-current assets. The audit of depreciation is probably the most complex area in practice as it is a judgemental area.

The audit of non-current assets could be examined in conjunction with using the work of an expert, as non-current assets are often subject to revaluations.

The audit procedures in this chapter have been expressed in terms of the relevant financial statement assertions.

Tangible non-current assets are physical assets held for **continuing use** in the business.

The following box outlines the key control objectives relating to tangible non-current assets:

Internal control considerations

- Acquisitions are authorised
- Disposals are authorised
- Proceeds are accounted for
- Security over non-current assets sufficient
- Non-current assets maintained properly
- Depreciation reviewed annually
- Is a register kept?

Completeness

Obtain a summary, reconcile it to last year's schedules. **Reconcile** the list of assets in the **general ledger** with those in the **non-current asset register** or list of assets. Obtain explanations for missing assets. Test some physical assets to ensure they are recorded.

Existence

Confirm that the company physically inspects all the assets in the register annually. **Inspect assets** (Do they exist? What's their condition? Are they in use?). Reconcile opening and closing motor vehicles by numbers as well as by value.

Accuracy, allocation and valuation

Verify valuation to **valuation certificate** (consider reasonableness of valuation). Check any **revaluation surplus** has been **correctly calculated**. Check that revaluations are updated regularly. Ensure **disclosure** correct.

Charges and commitments (rights and obligations)

Review statutory books for evidence of charges, examine post year-end invoices and board minutes for evidence of any capital commitments.

Ownership (rights and obligations)

Verify title to **land** by checking **title deeds/leases**. Obtain certificate from people holding deeds to confirm why they are held. Inspect **registration documents for vehicles**, confirm that they are **used for the business**. Examine documents of title for other assets.

Disposals (rights/completeness/occurrence)

Verify disposals to **sales documentation** (invoice) and verify **calculation of profit/loss** is correct. Verify that disposals are **authorised** and proceeds are reasonable. Ensure that asset is no longer used as security.

Additions (rights/valuation/completeness)

Verify additions to invoices/architect's certificates etc. Ensure purchases properly allocated to asset accounts and authorised by correct person and that all additions have been recorded in the general ledger and the asset register.

Depreciation (valuation)

Review depreciation rates in light of: asset lives, residual values, replacement policy, past experience (consistency), possible obsolescence. **Verify** that **depreciation has been charged** on all assets with a useful economic life. **Review calculation**. Ensure depreciation not charged on fully depreciated assets. Verify that rates and policies are disclosed in the FS. Confirm that depreciation on revalued assets is based on the revalued amount.

Insurance (valuation)

Review insurance policies in force for all assets to ensure cover is sufficient and verify expiry dates.

Key assertions: **Existence** → Are they genuinely assets?
Valuation → At what value should they be recorded?

Goodwill

- Agree consideration to sales agreement
- Asset values reasonable?
- Calculation correct?
- Amortisation correct?
- Any impairment?
- Goodwill valuation reasonable?

Intangibles

- Agree to purchase documentation
- Review any specialist valuations
- Amortisation correct?

R&D

- Conforms to IAS 38 criteria?
- Refer to budgets
- Amortisation correct?

13: Inventory

Topic List

The inventory count

Cut-off

Valuation

In practice, inventory is a very important audit area. For manufacturing businesses, it is often the largest item on the statement of financial position, and is usually material.

Inventory can be a difficult area to audit. It often comprises lots of small items, which can make it time consuming to audit. There are three key areas: the inventory count (existence), cut-off (completeness) and valuation.

Sources of rules on inventories

- IAS 2 *Inventories* (IAS2: para. 9) (lower of cost and NRV)
- ISA 501 *Audit Evidence – Specific Considerations for Selected Items*

Methods of valuation

- First in first out (FIFO)
- Weighted average cost
- Other similar methods

The inventory count

There are various methods:

- Inventory count at the year-end — The auditors' favourite
- Inventory count prior to/after the year-end
- Continuous inventory count

Responsibilities in relation to inventories

- **Management:** Ensure inventory figure in FS represents inventories that exists/is owned, keep inventory count records.
- **Auditors:** Obtain sufficient audit evidence about inventories, and attend inventory count if inventory is material.

Auditors must ensure that all inventory lines are counted annually, the inventory records are adequate and that management investigates all material differences.

Planning inventory count

Gain knowledge (previous year) and discuss major changes with management.

Assess key factors (such as, nature of inventories, high value items, accounting, location, controls).

Plan procedures (time/location of attendance, high value items, any specialist help, third party confirmations required?)

During inventory count

Observe whether **instructions** are followed.

Make **test counts** for accuracy.

Review procedures for **obsolete** inventories.

Confirm **third party** inventories separate.

Conclude whether inventory count has been **properly carried out.**

Gain overall **impression** of inventories.

Review inventory count instructions

Ensure there is provision for:

Organisation of count (supervision, marking of inventories, control during the process, identification of obsolete inventories).

Counting (systematic counting to ensure all inventories are counted, teams of two counters one independent of inventories usually). **Recording** (control over inventory sheets, ink used, signed by counters).

After inventory count

Trace **test count** items to final inventory sheets.

All count records **included** in final total?

Confirm **cut-off** using final goods in and out records.

Review replies from **third parties**.

Confirm **valuation**.

It is important that all inventory movements are recorded in the correct period.

Cut-off is critical at the following points in the accounting cycle:

- Point of purchase/receipt of goods
- Raw materials going to production
- Transfer of WIP to finished goods
- Sale/dispatch of finished goods

Purchase invoices should only be recorded as liabilities if goods were received prior to the inventory count.

Invoices for goods despatched after the inventory count should not appear in the statement of profit or loss for the year.

There are usually fewer problems with sales cut-off than purchase cut-off.

Cut-off procedures at inventory count

Record the relevant movements (last and first goods despatched and received numbers).

Observe whether cut-off procedures are being followed during count.

Discuss procedures with management.

Cut-off procedures at final audit

Match goods received notes with purchase invoices and goods despatched notes with sales invoices and ensure all in the **correct period**. Match materials requisitions with work in progress figures to ensure cut-off correct.

Remember: inventories should be valued at the lower of cost and net realisable value.

Original cost (All types of inventories)

The various methods of valuing inventories were outlined earlier. The auditors must ensure that the **method** is **allowed** under law and standards, **consistent, calculated correctly**.

Actual costs can be checked by referring to **supplier invoices**.

The auditor should bear in mind the **age** of inventories when considering cost.

Production cost (WIP and FG)

Cost is the cost of purchase + **cost of conversion**

The auditors may be able to use **analytical procedures** to assess the costs of conversion.

Material: verify to invoices and price lists.

Labour: verify to wage records/time summaries.

Overheads: allocation consistent and based on normal production.

NRV (All types of inventories)

Auditors should compare cost/ NRV. **NRV is likely to be lower** than **cost** where:

- Costs increasing
- Inventories deteriorated
- Inventories obsolete
- Marketing strategy dictates
- Errors made

The auditors should follow up **obsolete items** and **review prices** and strategies.

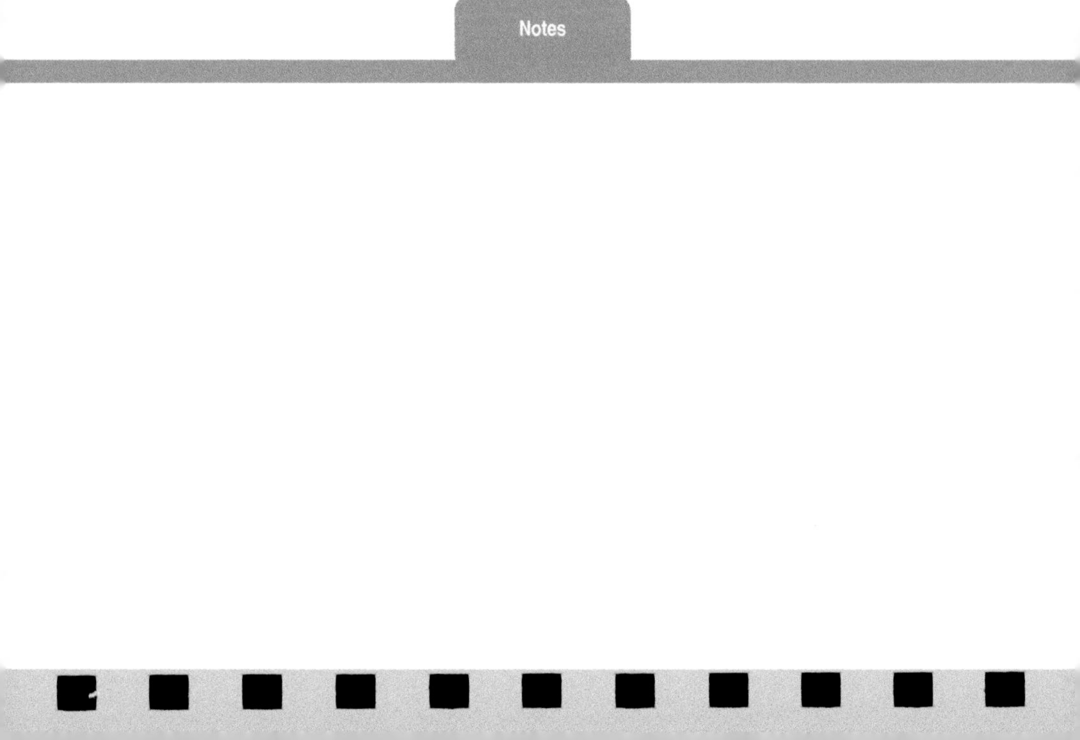

Notes

14: Receivables

Topic List

Receivables can be a significant asset on the statement of financial position. Customers are third parties to the business, so represent an important source of evidence to auditors. The circularisation of receivables provides good evidence about the existence of year-end receivables. Other audit evidence comes from cut-off testing, analytical procedures and the review of after-date cash.

Sales

Receivables will often be tested in conjunction with sales.

Completeness and occurrence

Analytical procedures are likely to be important.

Consider:

- Level of sales, year on year
- Effect of changing quantities sold
- Effect of changing prices
- Levels of goods returned/ discounts
- Efficiency of labour/sales

Accuracy

Check:

- Pricing/additions on invoices
- Discounts properly calculated
- Sales tax added correctly
- Casts in sales ledger
- Control account reconciliation

Also, trace debits in sales ledger to credit notes.

Sales cut-off

- Confirm goods in inventory are not also treated as sales in the year.

Review goods dispatched and returns inward around the year-end to ensure:

- Invoices/credit notes dated in the same period
- Invoices/credit notes posted to the sales ledger in the same period

Review the sales ledger control account for unusual items near the year-end and review material after-date invoices and credit notes to see if in correct period.

Receivables' listing/age analysis

Much of the detailed work will be carried out on a sample of **receivables' balances** chosen from a list of **sales ledger balances**. Ideally, this will be **aged**, showing amounts owed and from when they are owed. The following work should be done **(completeness/cut-off)**.

Audit work on receivables

Reconcile balances from sales ledger to list of balances and vice versa.

Reconcile the total of the list to the sales ledger control account.

Cast the list of balances to ensure it is correct.

Confirm whether the list reconciles to the sales ledger control account.

Circularisation

Verification of trade receivables by direct circularisation is the normal method of getting audit evidence to check the **existence** and **rights and obligations** of trade receivables. ISA 505 *External Confirmations* provides guidance.

Positive circularisation: customer is requested to confirm the accuracy of the balance shown or state in what respect he is in disagreement (preferable method). (ISA 505: para. 6)

Negative circularisation: customer is requested only to reply if the amount is disputed. (ISA 505: para. 6)

Auditors must maintain control over the preparation and dispatch of confirmation letters.

Sample selection

Special attention to:

- **Old** unpaid accounts
- Accounts **written-off** in period
- Accounts with **credit** balances
- Accounts settled by **round sum payments**

Do not overlook:

- **Nil balances**
- Accounts paid by the time of the audit

Follow up, where:

- Customers disagree with the balance
- Customers do not respond (positive method only)

(ISA 505: para. A7)

Reasons for disagreements: disputes, cut off problems, receipt sent before year-end but received afterwards, mis-posting, customers netting off credits and debits, teeming and lading frauds. The **auditors should investigate** the reasons for disagreement.

Alternative procedures (where no response arrives):

Second (and third) requests should be sent to the customer in the first instance. Then the auditors should involve the credit controller to chase the debt, and do other tests.

Auditor may check the receipt of cash after date, verify purchase orders, and test the company's control over bad debts (see below).

Irrecoverable debts

A test of the valuation of trade receivables in the statement of financial position. A significant test is reviewing all the **cash received after date** (which gives evidence on the **collectability** of debts).

Procedures

Confirm adequacy of allowance by **reviewing customer** correspondence/ discussion with the credit controller.

Examine customer files for overdue debts and consider whether allowance is sufficient.

Review correspondence with **solicitors** in case legal action is being taken to enforce debts.

Examine **credit notes** issued after the year-end and ensure those relating to invoices in the relevant period have been allowed for.

Investigate all **unusual items** in the sales ledger, for example, credit balances.

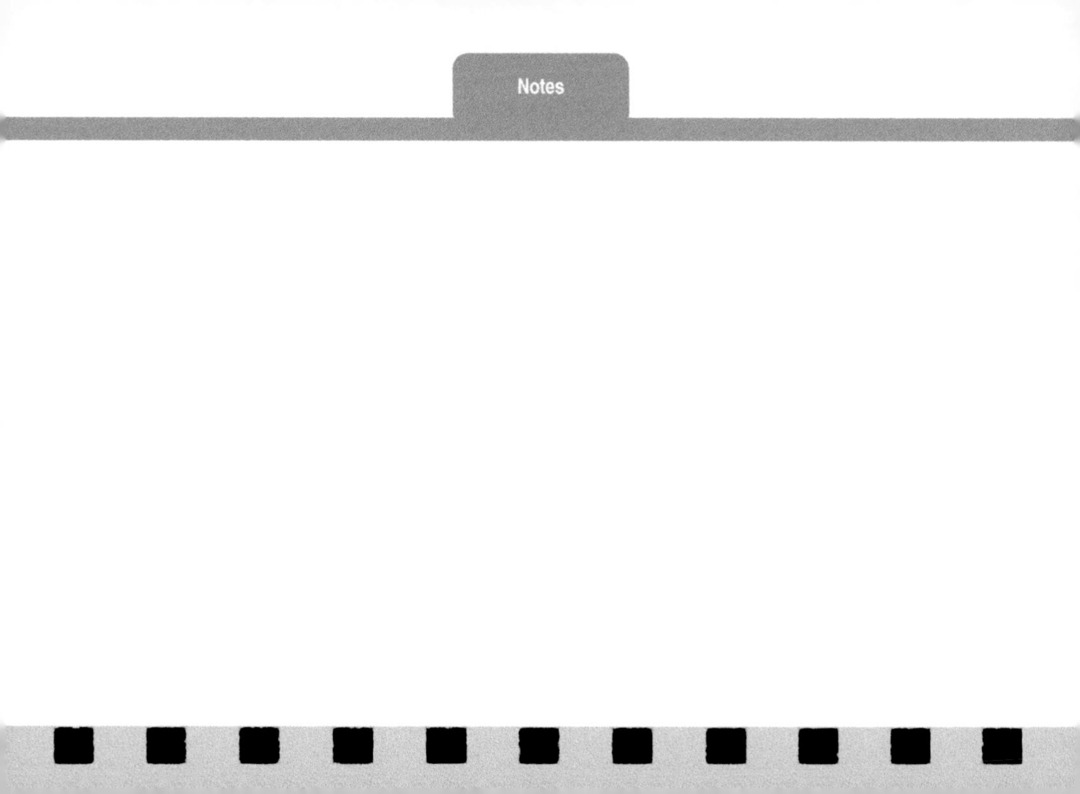
Notes

15: Cash and bank

Topic List

The bank reconciliation and bank confirmation letter are key parts of audit testing on bank. The direct confirmation from the bank represents good audit evidence. Auditors should be aware of the practice of 'window-dressing' if clients have liquidity problems.

This area of the syllabus is likely to appear in a short knowledge-based question, perhaps on the bank confirmation letter or in relation to the financial statement assertions.

The audit of bank and cash will need to cover **completeness, existence, rights and obligations**, accuracy, valuation and allocation and presentation.

All these elements can be audited through the **bank letter**. This is a standard document.

Banks will require:

- Explicit written authority from client
- Auditor's request must refer to it
- Request must reach the bank one month before the year end

Guidance is provided by:

- ISA 505 *External Confirmations*

Procedures

- Obtain bank confirmations
- Check the maths of the bank reconciliation
- Trace cheques shown as outstanding to the after date bank statements
- Trace receipts shown as outstanding to after date bank statements
- Review previous bank reconciliation to ensure all amounts are cleared
- Obtain explanations for items in bank statements, not cash book and vice versa
- Verify balances on reconciliation to bank letter and cash book
- Scrutinise the cash book for unusual items

If cash balances at the client are **material**, then the auditor may decide to attend a cash count.

Planning

Document on file: the time and location of the count, who is to be present (audit and client staff). Inspect the cash book to ensure it is written up to date and in ink.

During the cash count

Count cash balances held in front of official responsible. (The auditor should never be left alone with the cash.)

Enquire into any IOUs.

Confirm cash balances agree with the FS.

After the cash count

Ensure that certificates of cash in hand are obtained as appropriate.

Ensure unbanked cheques are subsequently banked/agree to bank reconciliation.

Ensure IOUs have been reimbursed.

Ensure IOUs/cashed cheques outstanding for too long have been provided for.

Ensure all balances counted are reflected in the accounts.

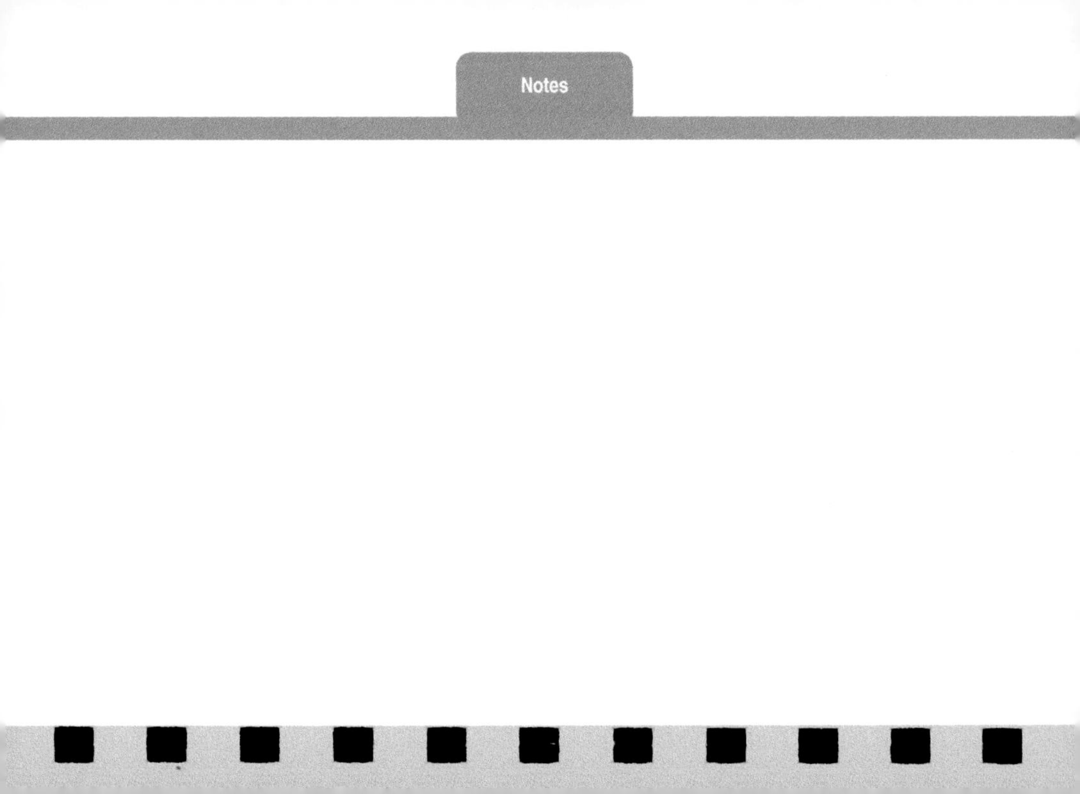
Notes

16: Liabilities, capital and directors' emoluments

Topic List

Trade accounts payable and purchases

Accruals

Long-term liabilities

Provisions and contingencies

Capital and directors' emoluments

This chapter covers a number of liabilities which a company might have. The auditor must consider the possibly of understatement of liabilities, particularly if the client has liquidity problems, or is seeking further credit from the bank, for example.

Suppliers and lenders are a good source of external evidence. Auditors may also test purchases by analytical review.

Capital and directors' emoluments are also covered in this chapter.

Auditors should be aware of the possibility of understatement of payables.

There are **two detailed objectives** with regard to trade accounts payable:

- Is cut-off correct between goods received and invoices received?
- Do trade accounts payable represent the *bona fide* amounts due by the company?

Trade accounts payable listing

- Confirm that the listing has been extracted correctly from the purchase ledger
- Reconcile the total with the purchase ledger control account
- Recast the list of balances

Completeness, rights and obligations, existence

The key test is a comparison of supplier statements with the purchase ledger balances. Supplier statements are third party evidence.

However, it is sometimes necessary to **circularise suppliers**. Examples of such situations are:

- Supplier statements are unavailable/incomplete.
- Internal controls are weak and material misstatement of liabilities is feared as a consequence.
- Suspicion that client is understating deliberately.

Purchases and expenses

Occurrence/completeness

Analytical procedures are important. Consider:

- Level of purchases/expenses month by month
- Effect of quantities purchased
- Effect of changing prices
- Ratio of purchases to trade payables
- Ratio of trade creditors to inventory

Additional tests include tracing purchases and other expenses from the nominal ledger to the purchase ledger and invoices. Are they valid for the company/authorised?

Cut-off (completeness)

Ensure goods from the **last goods received note** (from inventory count) are included in the ledger or list of accruals.

Review the **schedule of accruals** to check that goods received after the year-end are not included.

Review invoices and credit notes after the year-end to ensure that those relating to prior year are included.

Reconcile batch postings around the year-end, to ensure that invoices are posted in the correct period.

As a general rule, accruals lend themselves to being audited by analytical review as they should be comparable to prior years. Other substantive procedures are noted here.

General accruals

(completeness and valuation)

Recalculate accruals and trace back to supporting documentation.

Review ledger accounts to ensure all accruals have been included.

Scrutinise post year-end payments to see if any should have been accrued.

Consider basis for round sum accruals (comparable to last year?).

Tax accruals

(completeness and valuation)

Income tax: Agree to the previous period's tax change/credits, the current period's tax change, and amount paid to the tax authority.

Sales tax: Assess reasonableness to next return. Verify amount paid in year to cashbook.

Wages and salaries

(completeness and valuation)

Analytical procedures will give some assurance on pay liabilities. However, auditors may also carry out tests such as: agreeing remuneration per payroll to personnel records, confirm existence of employees by meeting them, re-perform calculations on the payroll, agree validity of deductions to supporting documentation, confirm net pay to bank.

Long-term liabilities are those due after more than one year. Usually they are debentures, loan stock and bank loans.

The key financial statement assertions are:

- **Completeness:** whether all long-term liabilities have been disclosed
- **Accuracy, valuation and allocation:** whether interest payable has been calculated correctly and included in the right period
- **Presentation:** whether long-term loans are correctly disclosed

Audit procedures

- Obtain/prepare a schedule of loans
- Agree opening balances to prior year and recast
- Compare the balances to the general ledger
- Verify lenders to any register of lenders (eg debenture holders)
- Trace additions and repayments to cash book
- Confirm repayment conforms to agreement
- Verify borrowing limits per the articles are not exceeded
- Obtain direct confirmation from lenders
- Review minutes and cash book to ensure that all loans have been included

Provisions and contingencies

A **provision** is a liability of uncertain timing or amount. A liability is a present obligation arising from past events, resulting in an outflow of resources. (IAS 37: para. 10)

A **contingent asset/liability** is a possible asset/liability arising from past events whose existence will be confirmed only by the occurrence of one of more uncertain future events not wholly within the entity's control, or (liability) a present obligation that arises from past events but is not probable that a transfer of economic benefits will be required, or the amount cannot be measured with reasonable certainty. (IAS 37: para. 10)

Auditing provisions/contingencies

- Obtain details of provisions/contingencies
- Review correspondence
- Discuss with directors
- Ascertain whether payments have been made in respect of provisions in the subsequent events period
- Review correspondence with solicitors pre and post year-end
- Consider past provisions – were they subsequently required?
- Recalculate all the provisions to ensure correct
- Ensure disclosures made about contingencies are complete and accurate
- Consider the nature of the client's business (would you expect to see other provisions – for example, for warranties?)

Share (equity) capital

Auditors should ensure that the directors have observed their legal duties in regard to share capital and reserves (for example, not distributed undistributable reserves).

- Agree authorised share capital to the memorandum
- Verify share transfer details and cash payments to cash book
- Agree dividends paid to cash book and to the minutes of the AGM where the dividend was proposed
- Check calculation of movement on reserves

Directors' emoluments

Auditors should ensure the disclosure of directors emoluments is complete, accurate and compliant with applicable accounting standards and local legislation.

- Agree details to payroll records
- Review directors' contracts
- Review minutes of board meetings

17: Not-for-profit organisations

Topic List

External and internal auditors might both have to carry out work in not-for-profit organisations. This chapter points out some special considerations when auditing such entities.

The auditing methods you have learned in the rest of your studies are still relevant to these types of audits: these are ***additional*** *considerations.*

Examples of NFPOs

A **charity** is a common form of not-for-profit organisation.

A charity is any institution established for charitable purposes and subject to the control of the law as such.

Charitable purposes includes:

- Relief of poverty
- Advancement of education
- Advancement of religion
- Purposes to benefit community

Accounts may include:

- Statement of financial activities (SOFA)
- In some cases a summary income and expenditure account
- Statement of financial position showing the assets, liabilities and funds of the charity
- Statement of cash flows (where required) and notes
- Auditors report on the truth and fairness of the FS
- Purposes to benefit community

Examples of NFPOs (continued)

Other NFPOs include:

- Tax payer funded organisations eg:
  - Hospitals
  - Schools
  - Public services
  - Local councils
- Clubs and associations
- Friendly societies

Regulatory requirements may mean the scope of the auditor's work is increased and there may be additional reporting requirements (eg disclosure of non-compliance with entity specific laws). However the audit is still carried out in accordance with ISAs.

Problem areas

- **Donations** (not supported by invoice/equivalent documentation)
- **Legacies** (income recognition)
- **Government funding** or **grants** (often subject to conditions)
- **Restricted funds** (uses are restricted as per deed/benefactor)
- **Grants to beneficiaries** (must be *bona fide*)
- **Branches** (charities' SORP requires inclusions in main accounts)

Planning

Auditors should consider:

- The **scope** of the audit
- Recommendations of **regulators**
- **Accounting policies**
- **Changes in the sector** in which the NFPO operates
- **Past experience** of the system
- **Key audit areas**
- **Detail** in FS on which auditors report
- **Risk**

Inherent risk

Factors include: complexity/extent of regulation, significance of donations and cash receipts, lack of predictable income, restricted funds, restrictions imposed by governing documents or the government, tax rules, sensitivity of key statistics, balance of maintaining resources/building up funds.

Control risk

Factors include: time committed and degree of involvement by trustees, skills of trustees, independence of trustees from each other, division of duties.

Control environment: segregation of duties a very key area in small NFPOs.

Internal controls

Problems can include:

- Lack of segregation of duties
- Use of unqualified staff

Example

Controls over cash donations

Source	*Examples of controls*
Collecting boxes and tins	■ Numerical control over boxes and tins ■ Satisfactory sealing of boxes and tins so that any opening prior to recording cash is apparent ■ Regular collecting and recording of proceeds ■ Dual control over counting and recording of proceeds ■ Postal receipts
Postal receipts	■ Unopened mail kept securely ■ Dual control over the opening of mail ■ Immediate recording of donations on opening of mail or receipt ■ Agreement of bank paying-in slips to record of receipts by an independent person

Audit evidence

- Consider **understatement/incompleteness** in **income**
- **Overstatement of grants or assets**
- Misanalysis or misuse of **funds**
- Misstatement of assets like **donated properties**
- Existence of restricted funds in foreign **branches**

Overall view

Consider if **accounting policies** are appropriate. **Analytical procedures** might be restricted due to lack of predictable income etc, but NFPOs should have budget or strategy information available.

Reporting

The form of the auditor's report is dictated by the NFPO's applicable legislation or charity's constitution but it should conform to ISA 700 criteria. The financial statements should have been prepared in accordance with any additional statutory requirements or specific guidance applicable to the NFPO. That fact should be referred to in the auditor's report.

Where NFPOs are not governed by statute, the auditor's report will depend upon the scope of the assignment.

18: Audit review and finalisation

Topic List

In this chapter we discuss subsequent events and the significance of the going concern concept and the importance of the auditor's going concern review. If the going concern basis is not appropriate, the financial statements will be materially affected.

We also discuss the need for written representations as audit evidence and the importance of the overall review of the financial statements.

Subsequent events are events occurring between the date of the financial statements and the date of the auditor's report, and facts that become known to the auditor after the date of the auditor's report. There are two types, those that provide evidence of conditions that existed at the period-end (**adjusting events**) and those that are indicative of conditions that arose subsequent to the period-end (**non-adjusting events**).

ISA 560 *Subsequent Events* provides guidance in this area.

Prior to the auditor's report being signed

Auditors shall carry out audit procedures to obtain evidence about subsequent events, including (ISA 560: paras. 6–9):

Audit procedures

- Inquiries of management
- Reading minutes of meetings of those charged with governance
- Reviewing most recent financial information
- Written representations

Examples: Inquiries of management (ISA 560: para. A9)

- Status of items involving subjective data included in the FS
- New commitments, borrowings, guarantees
- Sales or destruction of assets
- Issue of shares or debentures
- Unusual accounting adjustments
- Litigations or claims
- Major events

After the auditor's report has been signed

The auditors do **not** have any obligation to perform procedures, or make inquiries **after** the date of their report. (ISA 560: para. 10)

Before issued to members (ISA 560: paras. 10 & 13)

- Discuss with management and those charged with governance
- Determine if FS need amending
- If not amended and auditor's report not issued, modify opinion
- If not amended and auditor's report issued, prevent reliance on report

After issue (ISA 560: paras. 14–17)

- Discuss with management and those charged with governance
- Determine if FS need amending
- Review management's procedures to inform readers
- Issue new auditor's report with emphasis of matter paragraph
- If steps not taken, prevent reliance on report

Going concern: an entity is ordinarily viewed as continuing in business for the foreseeable future.

ISA 570 *Going Concern* gives guidance.

Auditor responsibilities

The auditors are responsible for obtaining sufficient appropriate audit evidence about the appropriateness of management's use of the going concern basis of accounting, and for considering whether there is a **material uncertainty** in relation to going concern. (ISA 570: para. 6)

Planning and risk assessment

When performing risk assessment procedures, the auditor shall consider whether anything casts doubt on the entity's going concern status. If management has undertaken a preliminary assessment of going concern, the auditor shall discuss it with management. If no assessment has been done yet, the auditor shall discuss with management the basis for the intended use of the going concern basis of accounting. The auditor shall remain alert throughout the audit for evidence of conditions or events that may cast doubt on the entity's ability to continue as a going concern. (ISA 570: paras. 10 & 11)

Examples

Financial

- Net liabilities
- Fixed term borrowing approaching maturity without realistic prospect of renewal/repayment
- Negative operating cash flows
- Adverse financial ratios
- Substantial operation losses
- Inability to pay creditors
- Inability to finance new products

Operating

- Loss of key management/markets/franchise
- Labour difficulties/supply shortage

Other

- Major legal proceedings/non-compliance
- Uninsured catastrophes

(ISA 570: para. A3)

Evaluation

The auditors shall consider:

- **Process** used by directors
- **Assumptions** used
- **Plans** for future action

Further procedures

- Analyse and discuss cash flow/profit/other forecasts/interim financial information with management
- Review the terms of debentures/loan agreements
- Read minutes of meetings, make inquiries of lawyers regarding legal claims
- Confirm financial support from third parties, consider unfulfilled orders
- Review events after the period-end

Reporting

The following table summarises the possible scenarios that could arise following the auditor's review of going concern. (ISA 570: paras. 21–24)

Scenario	Impact on auditor's report
Going concern basis of accounting appropriate but material uncertainty which is adequately disclosed	Unmodified opinion and material uncertainty related to going concern paragraph
Going concern basis of accounting appropriate but material uncertainty which is not adequately disclosed	Qualified or adverse opinion (ie modified)
Use of going concern basis of accounting inappropriate	Adverse opinion (ie modified)
Management unwilling to make or extend its assessment	Qualified or disclaimer of opinion (ie modified)

Written representations are written statements by management provided to the auditor to confirm certain matters or to support other audit evidence. They do not include the financial statements, assertions or supporting books and records.

Auditors receive many **representations** from management during the course of an audit, and **some may be critical** to obtaining sufficient appropriate audit evidence. An example, which the auditors must get, is acknowledgement from the directors of their responsibility for the financial statements which the auditors have audited.

Guidance is given in ISA 580 *Written Representations.*

Written representations

- That management believes it has fulfilled the fundamental responsibilities that constitute the premise on which an audit is conducted
- That management has provided the auditor with all relevant information agreed in the terms of the engagement
- That supports other audit evidence if determined necessary by the auditor or if required by other ISAs (ISA 580: paras. 10, 11 & 13)

Doubt about reliability

If representations are inconsistent with other evidence, the auditor shall perform audit procedures to resolve the matter. If it cannot be resolved, the auditor shall reconsider the assessment of the competence, integrity and ethical values of management, the reliability of representations and evidence, and the impact on the auditor's report.

(ISA 580: paras. 16–18)

Basic elements of a representation letter

- Addressed to the auditors
- Contains specified information
- Appropriately dated
- Approved by those with specific knowledge
- Signed by senior financial officer

Written representations not provided

The auditor shall discuss the matter with management, re-evaluate the integrity of management and take appropriate action. (ISA 580: para. 19)

Towards the end of their audit, the auditors should review the financial statements to ensure that they are reasonable, and consistent with evidence obtained, so that they can draw a conclusion on truth and fairness.

Compliance with accounting regulations

The auditors should **examine the accounting policies**, considering; what policies are usually adopted in the industry, whether there is substantial authoritative support for the policy, whether departures are necessary for a true and fair view, whether the FS reflect the substance of the underlying transactions.

Some accounting standards allow a **choice of methods**, which often have a material effect.

Review for consistency and reasonableness

1. Do FS adequately reflect **explanations** received?
2. Are there any **new factors** in presentation?
3. Do **analytical procedures** produce expected results?
4. Has the **presentation** been unduly affected by directors' wishes?
5. What is the potential impact of **uncorrected misstatements**?

Treatment of misstatements

A **misstatement** is a difference between the amount, classification, presentation or disclosure of a reported financial statement and the amount, classification, presentation or disclosure that is required for the item to be in accordance with the applicable financial reporting framework.

An **uncorrected misstatement** is a misstatement accumulated during the audit which has not been corrected.

(ISA 450: para. 4)

ISA 450 *Evaluation of Misstatements Identified During the Audit* provides guidance.

Types of misstatements

- Factual (no doubt)
- Judgemental (management's judgement concerning accounting estimates or accounting policies)
- Projected (auditor's best estimate)

ISA 450

The auditor must communicate all misstatements accumulated during the audit to the appropriate level of management on a timely basis and request them to be corrected. (ISA 450: para. 8)

The auditor must obtain a written representation that management believes the effects of uncorrected misstatements are immaterial to the financial statements as whole. (ISA 450: para. 14)

19: Reports

Topic List

In the exam you may be required to:

- *Identify and/or describe how a particular modification affects the auditor's report*
- *Comment on extracts from auditor's reports*

You should also be comfortable with the report to management as you may be required to draft extracts of the report for a particular scenario in the exam.

Basic elements of auditor's report

- Title
- Addressee
- Opinion paragraph
- Basis for opinion
- Going concern (where applicable)
- Key audit matters (for listed companies or where ISA 701 is adopted)

Basic elements of auditor's report

- Other information (where applicable)
- Responsibilities for the financial statements
- Auditor's responsibilities
- Other reporting responsibilities (if applicable)
- Auditor's signature
- Date of the auditor's report
- Auditor's address

(ISA 700: paras. 22–49)

In an auditor's report with an **unmodified** opinion, the auditor concludes that the financial statements are prepared, in all material respects, in accordance with the applicable financial reporting framework. (ISA 700: para. 16)

In our opinion, the financial statements present fairly, in all material respects, (or give a true and fair view of) the financial position of ABC Company as of December 31, 20X1, and (of) its financial performance and its cash flows for the year ended in accordance with International Financial Reporting Standards. (ISA 700: Appendix)

Modifications to the opinion in the auditor's report

ISA 705 *Modifications to the Opinion in the Independent Auditor's Report* deals with situations where the auditor cannot issue an unmodified opinion.

There are two circumstances under which the auditor's opinion will be modified. (ISA 705: para. 4)

1. The auditor concludes that the financial statements as a whole are **not free from material misstatement** (qualified opinion or adverse opinion).
2. The auditor is **unable to obtain sufficient appropriate audit evidence** to conclude that the financial statements as a whole are free from material misstatement (qualified opinion or disclaimer of opinion).

Exam focus

For a matter to affect the auditor's opinion it must be **material** to the financial statements.

Emphasis of matter paragraphs and other matter paragraphs

An **emphasis of matter paragraph** is included in the auditor's report to refer to a matter already appropriately presented or disclosed in the financial statements which is of such importance that it is fundamental to users' understanding of the financial statements. (ISA 706: para. 7)

Emphasis of matter paragraphs – examples

- Uncertainty relating to future outcome of exceptional litigation or regulatory action
- Early application of a new accounting standard that has a pervasive effect
- Major catastrophe that has a significant effect on financial position

An **other matter paragraph** is included in the auditor's report to refer to a matter other than those presented or disclosed which is relevant to users' understanding, or the auditor's responsibilities. (ISA 706: para. 7)

ISA 706 *Emphasis of Matter Paragraphs and Other Matter Paragraphs in the Independent Auditor's Report* provides guidance.

Other information is financial and non-financial information (other than the financial statements and the auditor's report thereon) included in an entity's annual report. (ISA 720: para. 12)

ISA 720 *The Auditor's Responsibilities Relating to Other Information* provides guidance.

Other information

Auditors shall review the other information for **material inconsistencies**. These may impact on the auditor's opinion on the financial statements. (ISA 720: para. 14)

Examples of other information

- Report by management on operations
- Financial summaries or highlights
- Employment data
- Planned capital expenditures
- Financial ratios
- Names of officers and directors
- Selected quarterly data

ISA 265 *Communicating Deficiencies in Internal Control to those Charged with Governance and Management* requires communication on various matters including deficiencies in control systems. This should be sent on a timely basis after the interim and final audits.

Format of the report to management

Deficiency → **Implication**  **Recommendation**

Exam focus

The report to management is a popular topic to examine in a scenario question. Your recommendations should be sensible and relevant, and you must always state the implications of the deficiencies identified.

Notes